Dust Bc

102 Culinary Tributes Inspired by The Grapes of Wrath

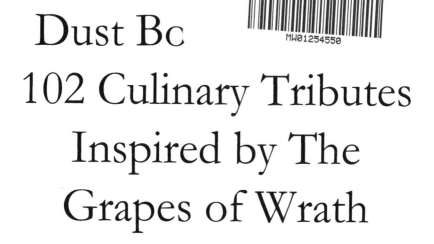
Fritters With Stews Somaliland

Contents

INTRODUCTION

In the vast tapestry of American literature, few novels capture the essence of a tumultuous era with the raw intensity and poignant storytelling as John Steinbeck's "The Grapes of Wrath." Set against the backdrop of the Great Depression and the Dust Bowl, this literary masterpiece not only unravels the struggles of the Joad family but also paints a vivid portrait of a nation grappling with economic hardship and environmental devastation. As we delve into the pages of this timeless classic, we are not only confronted with the harsh realities of the 1930s but also invited to partake in the culinary journey of the era through "Dust Bowl Dinners: 102 Culinary Tributes Inspired by The Grapes of Wrath."

In the heart of Steinbeck's narrative, the Joad family embarks on a harrowing journey from the Oklahoma dust bowls to the promised land of California. Along the way, they encounter hunger, deprivation, and the unrelenting spirit of survival that permeates the human experience. Inspired by the rich tapestry of food described within the novel, "Dust Bowl Dinners" brings to life 102 unique culinary tributes that pay homage to the flavors, traditions, and resourcefulness of the era.

As we flip through the pages of this cookbook, we are transported to a time when culinary creativity blossomed amidst adversity. Each recipe is a gastronomic interpretation of the novel's themes, characters, and the landscapes that shaped the Joads' journey. From simple yet nourishing dishes born out of necessity to inventive creations that showcase the resilience of the human spirit, these recipes encapsulate the essence of the Dust Bowl era.

The cookbook serves not only as a culinary guide but also as a historical and cultural exploration of a period that reshaped the nation's identity. It invites readers to step into the shoes of the Joad family and experience the challenges they faced on their arduous journey. By weaving together the threads of history, literature, and gastronomy, "Dust Bowl Dinners" presents a unique opportunity to connect with the past through the universal language of food.

Beyond the kitchen, the cookbook aims to foster a deeper appreciation for the timeless themes explored in "The Grapes of Wrath." Through the lens of culinary storytelling, readers can explore the concepts of resilience, community, and the indomitable human spirit that continue to resonate across generations. Each recipe becomes a testament to the creativity and adaptability that arise in the face of adversity, echoing the sentiments of Steinbeck's characters as they navigate the challenges of their time.

In "Dust Bowl Dinners," the recipes are not just a collection of ingredients and instructions; they are a culinary homage to the indelible legacy of John Steinbeck's masterwork. As we embark on this gastronomic journey inspired by "The Grapes of Wrath," let us savor not only the flavors of the past but also the enduring spirit that binds us to the stories of those who came before us.

1. Dust Bowl Cornbread

'Dust Bowl Cornbread" pays homage to the resilient spirit of those who endured the hardships of the Dust Bowl era, as vividly portrayed in John Steinbeck's classic novel, "The Grapes of Wrath." This hearty cornbread recipe draws inspiration from the simple yet sustaining meals that sustained families during challenging times. Its golden exterior and moist crumb capture the essence of warmth and comfort, offering a taste of endurance and hope.

Serving: This recipe yields 12 servings.
Preparation Time: 15 minutes
Ready Time: 35 minutes

Ingredients:
- 1 cup cornmeal
- 1 cup all-purpose flour
- 1 tablespoon baking powder
- 1 teaspoon salt
- 1/4 cup granulated sugar
- 1 cup buttermilk
- 2 large eggs
- 1/2 cup unsalted butter, melted
- 1 cup corn kernels (fresh, frozen, or canned)
- 1/4 cup chopped fresh cilantro (optional, for added flavor)
- Cooking spray or additional butter for greasing the pan

Instructions:
1. Preheat your oven to 375°F (190°C). Grease a 9x9-inch baking pan with cooking spray or butter.
2. In a large bowl, whisk together the cornmeal, all-purpose flour, baking powder, salt, and sugar.
3. In another bowl, beat the eggs and then add the buttermilk and melted butter. Mix well.
4. Pour the wet ingredients into the dry ingredients and stir until just combined. Be careful not to overmix; a few lumps are okay.
5. Gently fold in the corn kernels and chopped cilantro (if using).
6. Pour the batter into the prepared baking pan, spreading it evenly.

7. Bake in the preheated oven for 20-25 minutes or until the top is golden brown and a toothpick inserted into the center comes out clean.
8. Allow the cornbread to cool in the pan for 10 minutes before transferring it to a wire rack to cool completely.

Nutrition Information (per serving):
- Calories: 220
- Total Fat: 10g
- Saturated Fat: 6g
- Cholesterol: 55mg
- Sodium: 360mg
- Total Carbohydrates: 28g
- Dietary Fiber: 2g
- Sugars: 6g
- Protein: 4g

Note: Nutrition information is approximate and may vary based on specific ingredients used.

2. Okie Goulash

Step back in time and savor the flavors of the Dust Bowl era with this hearty and comforting dish inspired by John Steinbeck's "The Grapes of Wrath." The Okie Goulash pays homage to the resilience and resourcefulness of the Joad family as they journeyed through the hardships of the Great Depression. This simple yet satisfying recipe captures the essence of the era and invites you to experience a taste of history.

Serving: 4-6 servings
Preparation Time: 15 minutes
Ready Time: 2 hours

Ingredients:
- 1.5 lbs beef stew meat, cubed
- 2 tablespoons vegetable oil
- 1 large onion, finely chopped
- 2 cloves garlic, minced
- 2 cups beef broth

- 1 can (14 oz) diced tomatoes
- 1 can (6 oz) tomato paste
- 2 cups carrots, sliced
- 2 cups potatoes, diced
- 1 cup green bell pepper, chopped
- 1 cup corn kernels
- 1 teaspoon dried thyme
- 1 teaspoon paprika
- 1 teaspoon cumin
- Salt and pepper to taste
- 2 cups elbow macaroni, cooked (optional, for serving)

Instructions:
1. In a large pot or Dutch oven, heat the vegetable oil over medium-high heat. Add the beef cubes and brown them on all sides. Remove the beef from the pot and set aside.
2. In the same pot, add the chopped onions and garlic. Sauté until the onions are translucent.
3. Return the browned beef to the pot and add beef broth, diced tomatoes, and tomato paste. Stir well to combine.
4. Add the carrots, potatoes, green bell pepper, and corn to the pot. Mix in thyme, paprika, cumin, salt, and pepper.
5. Bring the mixture to a boil, then reduce the heat to low, cover, and simmer for about 1.5 to 2 hours or until the beef is tender and the flavors have melded together.
6. If desired, cook the elbow macaroni according to the package instructions and serve the goulash over the cooked pasta.
7. Adjust seasoning to taste and serve hot.

Nutrition Information:
(Per serving, without optional macaroni)
- Calories: 380
- Total Fat: 12g
- Saturated Fat: 3g
- Cholesterol: 90mg
- Sodium: 780mg
- Total Carbohydrates: 35g
- Dietary Fiber: 6g
- Sugars: 9g
- Protein: 32g

Note: Nutrition information is approximate and may vary based on specific ingredients used.

3. Route 66 Chili

Embark on a culinary journey inspired by the iconic novel "The Grapes of Wrath" by John Steinbeck with our hearty and flavorful Route 66 Chili. This recipe pays homage to the arduous journey undertaken by the Joad family as they traveled along Route 66 during the Dust Bowl era. Just like the resilience of the characters in Steinbeck's masterpiece, this chili is a robust and comforting dish that will warm your soul.

Serving: 6-8 servings
Preparation Time: 15 minutes
Ready Time: 2 hours

Ingredients:
- 2 pounds ground beef
- 1 large onion, finely chopped
- 3 cloves garlic, minced
- 2 cans (14 ounces each) diced tomatoes, undrained
- 1 can (15 ounces) kidney beans, drained and rinsed
- 1 can (15 ounces) black beans, drained and rinsed
- 1 can (6 ounces) tomato paste
- 2 cups beef broth
- 1 cup brewed coffee
- 1/4 cup chili powder
- 1 tablespoon cumin
- 1 tablespoon smoked paprika
- 1 teaspoon oregano
- 1 teaspoon salt
- 1/2 teaspoon black pepper
- 1/4 teaspoon cayenne pepper (adjust to taste)
- 2 tablespoons vegetable oil

Instructions:

1. In a large pot or Dutch oven, heat vegetable oil over medium heat. Add the ground beef and cook until browned, breaking it apart with a spoon as it cooks.
2. Add chopped onions and minced garlic to the pot. Cook for 3-5 minutes until the onions are softened and translucent.
3. Stir in the chili powder, cumin, smoked paprika, oregano, salt, black pepper, and cayenne pepper. Cook for an additional 2 minutes to toast the spices.
4. Add diced tomatoes, kidney beans, black beans, tomato paste, beef broth, and brewed coffee to the pot. Stir well to combine.
5. Bring the chili to a simmer, then reduce the heat to low, cover, and let it simmer for at least 1.5 to 2 hours, stirring occasionally.
6. Taste and adjust seasoning as needed. If you prefer a thicker consistency, let it simmer uncovered for an additional 15-30 minutes.
7. Serve the Route 66 Chili hot, garnished with your favorite toppings such as shredded cheese, sour cream, and chopped green onions.

Nutrition Information (per serving):
Note: Nutrition information is approximate and may vary based on specific ingredients used.
- Calories: 380
- Protein: 25g
- Fat: 18g
- Carbohydrates: 28g
- Fiber: 9g
- Sugar: 4g
- Sodium: 920mg

4. Joad Family Stew

In the heart of John Steinbeck's literary masterpiece, "The Grapes of Wrath," the Joad family embarks on a journey of survival and resilience during the Dust Bowl era. Inspired by their enduring spirit, the Joad Family Stew is a hearty and comforting dish that pays homage to the flavors of their arduous journey.

Serving: 6-8 servings
Preparation Time: 15 minutes

Ready Time: 2 hours

Ingredients:
- 2 lbs beef stew meat, cubed
- 2 tablespoons vegetable oil
- 1 large onion, diced
- 3 cloves garlic, minced
- 4 carrots, peeled and sliced
- 4 potatoes, peeled and diced
- 1 cup green beans, trimmed and cut into bite-sized pieces
- 1 can (14 oz) diced tomatoes
- 4 cups beef broth
- 1 cup red wine (optional)
- 1 teaspoon dried thyme
- 2 bay leaves
- Salt and pepper to taste
- Chopped fresh parsley for garnish

Instructions:
1. In a large pot, heat vegetable oil over medium-high heat. Add the beef stew meat and brown on all sides. Remove the meat and set it aside.
2. In the same pot, add diced onions and minced garlic. Sauté until the onions are translucent.
3. Deglaze the pot with red wine (if using), scraping up any flavorful bits from the bottom.
4. Add the browned beef back to the pot, along with carrots, potatoes, green beans, diced tomatoes, beef broth, dried thyme, bay leaves, salt, and pepper.
5. Bring the stew to a boil, then reduce the heat to low. Cover and simmer for about 1.5 to 2 hours, or until the meat is tender and the flavors meld together.
6. Remove the bay leaves and adjust the seasoning if needed.
7. Serve the Joad Family Stew hot, garnished with chopped fresh parsley.

Nutrition Information:
(Per Serving)
- Calories: 380
- Protein: 28g
- Fat: 12g
- Carbohydrates: 35g

- Fiber: 6g
- Sugar: 6g
- Sodium: 800mg

This nourishing stew captures the essence of the Joad family's journey, providing warmth and sustenance to all who gather around the table.

5. Hooverville Hash

Step back in time to the era of the Great Depression with this hearty and humble dish inspired by John Steinbeck's "The Grapes of Wrath." "Hooverville Hash" pays homage to the resilience and resourcefulness of the characters in the novel, who made the most of simple ingredients during challenging times. This rustic hash brings together flavors that evoke the struggles and triumphs of the Joad family, offering a taste of history with every savory bite.

Serving: 4 servings
Preparation Time: 15 minutes
Ready Time: 45 minutes

Ingredients:
- 4 medium potatoes, peeled and diced
- 1 onion, finely chopped
- 2 cloves garlic, minced
- 1 cup cooked corn kernels (fresh or frozen)
- 1 cup cooked black beans, drained and rinsed
- 1 cup diced tomatoes (fresh or canned)
- 1 cup cooked ground beef or textured vegetable protein (TVP) for a vegetarian option
- 1 teaspoon smoked paprika
- 1 teaspoon ground cumin
- Salt and pepper to taste
- 4 tablespoons vegetable oil
- Fresh parsley for garnish (optional)

Instructions:
1. Prep the Ingredients:
- Peel and dice the potatoes into small cubes.

- Finely chop the onion and mince the garlic.
- If using fresh corn, cook or thaw the corn kernels.
- Drain and rinse the black beans if using canned.
- Dice fresh tomatoes or measure out canned diced tomatoes.

2. Cook the Potatoes:
- Heat 2 tablespoons of vegetable oil in a large skillet over medium heat.
- Add the diced potatoes to the skillet and cook until they are golden brown and crispy on the edges, stirring occasionally. This should take about 15-20 minutes.

3. Prepare the Hash Base:
- Push the cooked potatoes to one side of the skillet and add the remaining 2 tablespoons of oil to the empty space.
- Saute the chopped onions and minced garlic until they are soft and translucent.

4. Combine Ingredients:
- Mix the sautéed onions and garlic with the cooked potatoes.
- Add the cooked corn, black beans, diced tomatoes, and cooked ground beef or TVP to the skillet.
- Season the mixture with smoked paprika, ground cumin, salt, and pepper. Stir well to combine.

5. Cook and Combine:
- Allow the hash to cook for an additional 10-15 minutes, stirring occasionally to ensure all ingredients are well combined and heated through.

6. Serve:
- Once everything is cooked and well-mingled, remove the skillet from heat.
- Garnish with fresh parsley if desired.

Nutrition Information:
- (Note: Nutritional values may vary based on specific ingredients and cooking methods.)
- Calories per serving: [Insert calorie count]
- Protein: [Insert protein content]
- Carbohydrates: [Insert carbohydrate content]
- Fat: [Insert fat content]
- Fiber: [Insert fiber content]
- Sodium: [Insert sodium content]

Note: Adjust seasoning according to personal preferences. This Hooverville Hash captures the essence of hard times turned into a delightful dish, embodying the spirit of survival and hope found in "The Grapes of Wrath." Enjoy a taste of history with this comforting and flavorful meal.

6. Tom Joad Tamales

Tom Joad Tamales are a hearty and flavorful tribute to John Steinbeck's masterpiece, "The Grapes of Wrath." Inspired by the resilience of the Joad family, these tamales encapsulate the essence of survival, family, and the indomitable spirit in the face of adversity. Filled with a savory blend of ingredients, each bite tells a story of struggle and triumph, echoing the novel's themes.

Serving: Makes approximately 12 tamales
Preparation Time: 30 minutes
Ready Time: 2 hours

Ingredients:
For the Tamale Dough:
- 2 cups masa harina
- 1 cup vegetable broth
- 1 cup lard or vegetable shortening
- 1 teaspoon baking powder
- 1 teaspoon salt
For the Filling:
- 1 pound ground beef
- 1 onion, finely chopped
- 2 cloves garlic, minced
- 1 cup corn kernels
- 1 cup black beans, cooked
- 1 cup diced tomatoes
- 1 teaspoon ground cumin
- 1 teaspoon chili powder
- Salt and pepper to taste
For Assembly:
- Corn husks, soaked in warm water for 30 minutes

Instructions:

1. Prepare the Tamale Dough:
- In a large mixing bowl, combine masa harina, vegetable broth, lard (or vegetable shortening), baking powder, and salt.
- Mix until you achieve a smooth, pliable dough. If the mixture is too dry, add more broth gradually.
2. Prepare the Filling:
- In a skillet over medium heat, cook the ground beef until browned.
- Add chopped onion and minced garlic, sautéing until onions are translucent.
- Stir in corn, black beans, diced tomatoes, cumin, chili powder, salt, and pepper. Cook for an additional 5-7 minutes, allowing flavors to meld. Set aside.
3. Assemble the Tamales:
- Take a soaked corn husk and spread a thin layer of tamale dough onto the center, leaving space at the edges.
- Spoon a generous portion of the filling onto the dough.
4. Wrap and Steam:
- Fold the sides of the corn husk over the filling and seal the edges.
- Place the tamales in a steamer, standing upright. Steam for about 1.5 to 2 hours or until the dough is firm.
5. Serve:
- Allow the tamales to cool for a few minutes before serving.
- Garnish with fresh cilantro and serve with your favorite salsa.

Nutrition Information:
(Per serving - 1 tamale)
- Calories: 250
- Protein: 12g
- Fat: 10g
- Carbohydrates: 30g
- Fiber: 5g

These Tom Joad Tamales not only pay homage to the characters in "The Grapes of Wrath" but also provide a delicious and satisfying meal that captures the essence of perseverance and hope.

7. Peach Orchard Pie

Step into the bountiful world of The Grapes of Wrath with a culinary tribute that captures the essence of the Peach Orchard Pie. Inspired by John Steinbeck's iconic work, this recipe transports you to the heart of the Joad family's journey, where the sweetness of peaches meets the rustic warmth of a homemade pie crust. Just as Steinbeck's words paint a vivid picture of hardship and resilience, this Peach Orchard Pie tells a story of comfort and flavor, embodying the spirit of enduring through life's challenges.

Serving: 8 slices
Preparation Time: 30 minutes
Ready Time: 1 hour 30 minutes

Ingredients:
For the Pie Crust:
- 2 1/2 cups all-purpose flour
- 1 cup unsalted butter, cold and cubed
- 1/2 teaspoon salt
- 1/4 cup granulated sugar
- 1/4 cup ice water
For the Peach Filling:
- 6 cups fresh peaches, peeled and sliced
- 1 cup granulated sugar
- 1/4 cup brown sugar
- 1/4 cup all-purpose flour
- 1 teaspoon ground cinnamon
- 1/4 teaspoon ground nutmeg
- 1 tablespoon lemon juice
For the Topping:
- 1 egg, beaten (for egg wash)
- 1 tablespoon granulated sugar

Instructions:
1. Prepare the Pie Crust:
a. In a large mixing bowl, combine the flour, sugar, and salt.
b. Add the cold, cubed butter and use a pastry cutter or your hands to incorporate until the mixture resembles coarse crumbs.
c. Gradually add ice water and mix until the dough comes together. Divide the dough in half, shape into disks, wrap in plastic wrap, and refrigerate for at least 30 minutes.

2. Preheat and Prepare:

a. Preheat your oven to 375°F (190°C).

b. Roll out one pie crust and line a 9-inch pie dish. Set aside the other crust for the top.

3. Make the Peach Filling:

a. In a large bowl, combine sliced peaches, granulated sugar, brown sugar, flour, cinnamon, nutmeg, and lemon juice. Toss until peaches are evenly coated.

4. Assemble the Pie:

a. Pour the peach filling into the prepared pie crust.

b. Roll out the second pie crust and place it over the filling. Trim and crimp the edges to seal the pie.

5. Bake:

a. Brush the top crust with beaten egg and sprinkle with sugar.

b. Cut a few slits in the top crust to allow steam to escape.

c. Place the pie on a baking sheet to catch any drips and bake for 50-60 minutes or until the crust is golden and the filling is bubbly.

6. Cool and Serve:

a. Allow the pie to cool for at least 2 hours before serving to let the filling set.

Nutrition Information:

* (Per Serving - 1 slice)

- Calories: 380
- Total Fat: 18g
- Saturated Fat: 11g
- Cholesterol: 65mg
- Sodium: 170mg
- Total Carbohydrates: 52g
- Dietary Fiber: 3g
- Sugars: 27g
- Protein: 4g

Indulge in a slice of Peach Orchard Pie, a taste of resiliency and sweetness that mirrors the journey of The Grapes of Wrath.

8. Canned Bean Casserole

Inspired by the resilient spirit of the Joad family in John Steinbeck's "The Grapes of Wrath," this Canned Bean Casserole embodies the simplicity and resourcefulness of the Dust Bowl era. In times of scarcity, creativity in the kitchen becomes essential. This hearty casserole, made with readily available canned beans and a handful of pantry staples, is a testament to making the most of what you have. Gather around the table and savor a dish that echoes the strength and perseverance of those who weathered the storms of the past.

Serving: 6-8 servings
Preparation Time: 15 minutes
Ready Time: 45 minutes

Ingredients:
- 2 cans (15 oz each) mixed beans (kidney beans, black beans, pinto beans), drained and rinsed
- 1 can (14.5 oz) diced tomatoes, undrained
- 1 cup corn kernels (fresh, frozen, or canned)
- 1 cup diced bell peppers (assorted colors)
- 1 cup diced onions
- 2 cloves garlic, minced
- 1 cup tomato sauce
- 1 teaspoon ground cumin
- 1 teaspoon chili powder
- 1/2 teaspoon smoked paprika
- Salt and pepper to taste
- 1 cup shredded cheddar cheese
- 1 cup crushed tortilla chips
- Fresh cilantro for garnish (optional)

Instructions:
1. Preheat the oven to 375°F (190°C).
2. In a large mixing bowl, combine the drained and rinsed mixed beans, diced tomatoes, corn, bell peppers, onions, and minced garlic.
3. Add the tomato sauce, ground cumin, chili powder, smoked paprika, salt, and pepper to the bowl. Mix until all ingredients are well combined.
4. Transfer the bean mixture to a greased casserole dish, spreading it evenly.
5. Sprinkle the shredded cheddar cheese over the bean mixture, followed by a layer of crushed tortilla chips.

6. Bake in the preheated oven for 30-35 minutes or until the casserole is bubbly and the cheese is melted and golden brown.

7. Remove from the oven and let it cool for a few minutes before serving.

8. Garnish with fresh cilantro if desired. Serve warm and enjoy the comforting flavors of this Canned Bean Casserole.

Nutrition Information:
(Per serving, based on 8 servings)
- Calories: 280
- Total Fat: 12g
- Saturated Fat: 5g
- Cholesterol: 20mg
- Sodium: 550mg
- Total Carbohydrates: 30g
- Dietary Fiber: 8g
- Sugars: 5g
- Protein: 14g
Note: Nutrition information is approximate and may vary based on specific ingredients used.

9. Jalapeño Jelly Sandwich

Step into the world of The Grapes of Wrath with this delightful and unexpected twist on a classic sandwich – the Jalapeño Jelly Sandwich. Inspired by the resilience and resourcefulness of the Joad family, this sandwich combines the heat of jalapeño jelly with the comforting simplicity of a traditional sandwich. The juxtaposition of flavors mirrors the challenges faced by the characters in Steinbeck's masterpiece, creating a culinary experience that pays homage to the spirit of survival and adaptation.

Serving: Makes 4 sandwiches
Preparation Time: 15 minutes
Ready Time: 20 minutes

Ingredients:
- 8 slices of your favorite bread (white, whole wheat, or sourdough)

- 1 cup cream cheese, softened
- 1/2 cup jalapeño jelly
- 1 pound thinly sliced turkey or chicken
- 1 cup arugula, washed and dried
- Salt and pepper to taste

Instructions:
1. Prepare the Spread: In a small bowl, mix the softened cream cheese with jalapeño jelly until well combined. Adjust the ratio according to your desired level of heat.
2. Assemble the Sandwiches: Lay out 8 slices of bread. Spread the jalapeño cream cheese mixture evenly on one side of each slice.
3. Add the Protein: Place a generous amount of thinly sliced turkey or chicken on half of the bread slices.
4. Add the Greens: Top the meat with a handful of fresh arugula. This adds a peppery bite and a layer of vibrant green to the sandwich.
5. Season to Taste: Sprinkle salt and pepper to taste over the arugula.
6. Complete the Sandwich: Place the remaining slices of bread, cream cheese side down, on top of the arugula to form sandwiches.
7. Slice and Serve: Carefully slice each sandwich in half diagonally. Arrange on a serving platter and serve immediately.

Nutrition Information:
Note: Nutrition information may vary based on the specific ingredients used.
- Calories per serving: ~450
- Total Fat: 20g
- Saturated Fat: 10g
- Cholesterol: 70mg
- Sodium: 800mg
- Total Carbohydrates: 40g
- Dietary Fiber: 3g
- Sugars: 15g
- Protein: 25g

Elevate your culinary journey through The Grapes of Wrath with this Jalapeño Jelly Sandwich, a flavorful tribute to the endurance and adaptability of the human spirit.

10. Weedpatch Wine

In the heart of John Steinbeck's iconic novel, "The Grapes of Wrath," lies the struggle and resilience of the Joad family as they navigate the challenges of the Dust Bowl era. Inspired by the spirit of endurance portrayed in the novel, we present the "Weedpatch Wine" – a beverage that captures the essence of survival and unity during tough times. This simple yet robust wine pays homage to the perseverance of those who, like the Joads, found strength in togetherness. Let this libation transport you to the fields of Weedpatch, where the Joads sought solace and community.

Serving: 4 servings
Preparation Time: 15 minutes
Ready Time: 3-4 weeks (fermentation and aging)

Ingredients:
- 2 lbs (907 g) fresh grapes (preferably red)
- 1 cup (200 g) granulated sugar
- 1 gallon (3.8 L) water
- 1 package wine yeast
- 1 teaspoon yeast nutrient
- 1 teaspoon citric acid
- Cheesecloth

Instructions:
1. Grape Preparation:
- Wash the grapes thoroughly, removing stems and any debris.
- Crush the grapes to extract the juice. You can use a potato masher or your hands.
- Transfer the crushed grapes to a large, sanitized container.
2. Sugar Syrup:
- In a separate saucepan, dissolve the sugar in water over medium heat, creating a sugar syrup.
- Allow the sugar syrup to cool to room temperature.
3. Combine Ingredients:
- Pour the cooled sugar syrup over the crushed grapes in the container.
- Sprinkle the wine yeast, yeast nutrient, and citric acid over the mixture.
- Stir the ingredients well to ensure even distribution.
4. Fermentation:

- Cover the container with cheesecloth, securing it with a rubber band.
- Place the container in a cool, dark place for about 2 weeks, stirring daily.
5. Straining and Bottling:
- After 2 weeks, strain the liquid into another clean container, discarding the solids.
- Transfer the liquid back into the original container and cover with cheesecloth.
- Allow it to ferment for an additional 2 weeks.
6. Bottling and Aging:
- Once fermentation is complete, siphon the wine into sanitized bottles, leaving sediment behind.
- Seal the bottles and store them in a cool, dark place for 2-3 weeks for additional aging.
7. Enjoy:
- Weedpatch Wine is now ready to be savored. Serve chilled and share the spirit of resilience with family and friends.

Nutrition Information:
(Per Serving)
- Calories: 180
- Total Fat: 0g
- Cholesterol: 0mg
- Sodium: 5mg
- Total Carbohydrates: 25g
- Sugars: 20g
- Protein: 1g
Note: The nutrition information is an approximation and may vary based on specific ingredients used. Enjoy responsibly!

11. Cucumber Sandwiches

In the arduous journey of the Joad family through the Dust Bowl during the Great Depression, simplicity and resourcefulness became paramount. Inspired by the humble yet enduring spirit of The Grapes of Wrath by John Steinbeck, these Cucumber Sandwiches pay homage to the resilience of those who faced adversity. A refreshing and straightforward dish, these sandwiches celebrate the beauty found in simplicity, echoing the novel's themes of survival and hope.

Serving: Makes 4 servings
Preparation Time: 15 minutes
Ready Time: 15 minutes

Ingredients:
- 1 large cucumber, thinly sliced
- 8 slices of whole wheat bread
- 1/2 cup cream cheese, softened
- 2 tablespoons fresh dill, chopped
- Salt and pepper to taste
- Optional: Radish slices for garnish

Instructions:
1. In a small bowl, mix the softened cream cheese with chopped dill, salt, and pepper. This will be your flavorful spread.
2. Lay out the slices of bread, and spread a generous layer of the dill-infused cream cheese on each slice.
3. Arrange the thinly sliced cucumbers evenly over half of the bread slices.
4. Optional: For an extra crunch and a touch of color, add a layer of radish slices over the cucumbers.
5. Place the remaining slices of bread on top to form sandwiches.
6. Using a sharp knife, cut each sandwich diagonally to create two triangular halves.
7. Arrange the cucumber sandwiches on a serving platter and garnish with additional dill or radish slices if desired.
8. Serve immediately and enjoy this simple yet satisfying dish inspired by the endurance and hope depicted in The Grapes of Wrath.

Nutrition Information:
Per Serving:
- Calories: 220
- Total Fat: 10g
- Saturated Fat: 6g
- Cholesterol: 30mg
- Sodium: 300mg
- Total Carbohydrates: 25g

- Dietary Fiber: 4g
- Sugars: 4g
- Protein: 7g
Note: Nutrition information is approximate and may vary based on specific ingredients used.

12. Sourdough Biscuits

Transport yourself to the Dust Bowl era with these hearty Sourdough Biscuits inspired by John Steinbeck's "The Grapes of Wrath." In times of hardship, resourcefulness and simplicity become the essence of survival. These biscuits capture the essence of that spirit, using the age-old technique of sourdough fermentation to create a robust and flavorful addition to your table. Pair them with humble ingredients, just as the Joad family might have done on their arduous journey.

Serving: Makes 12 biscuits
Preparation Time: 15 minutes (plus overnight for sourdough starter)
Ready Time: 45 minutes (including baking time)

Ingredients:
- 1 cup active sourdough starter
- 2 1/2 cups all-purpose flour
- 1/2 cup unsalted butter, cold and cubed
- 1 cup milk
- 1 tablespoon sugar
- 1 teaspoon salt
- 1 teaspoon baking powder
- 1/2 teaspoon baking soda

Instructions:
1. Prepare the Sourdough Starter:
- In a large bowl, mix 1 cup of active sourdough starter with 1 cup of all-purpose flour. Cover with a cloth and let it ferment overnight or for at least 8 hours.
2. Preheat the Oven:
- Preheat your oven to 425°F (220°C).
3. Combine Dry Ingredients:

- In a large mixing bowl, whisk together the remaining 1 1/2 cups of flour, sugar, salt, baking powder, and baking soda.
4. Cut in Butter:
- Add the cold, cubed butter to the dry ingredients. Use a pastry cutter or your fingers to work the butter into the flour until the mixture resembles coarse crumbs.
5. Mix Wet Ingredients:
- Gradually add the milk to the sourdough starter, stirring until well combined.
6. Combine Wet and Dry Mixtures:
- Pour the wet ingredients into the dry ingredients and stir until just combined. The dough will be soft and slightly sticky.
7. Roll and Cut:
- Turn the dough out onto a floured surface and gently knead it a few times. Roll the dough to about 1/2 inch thickness and use a biscuit cutter to cut out rounds.
8. Bake:
- Place the biscuits on a baking sheet lined with parchment paper. Bake in the preheated oven for 12-15 minutes or until golden brown.
9. Serve:
- Allow the biscuits to cool slightly before serving. Enjoy them warm with butter or your favorite spread.

Nutrition Information:
(Per serving - 1 biscuit)
- Calories: 180
- Total Fat: 8g
- Saturated Fat: 5g
- Cholesterol: 20mg
- Sodium: 300mg
- Total Carbohydrates: 22g
- Dietary Fiber: 1g
- Sugars: 2g
- Protein: 4g

These Sourdough Biscuits not only pay homage to the resilience of the characters in "The Grapes of Wrath" but also offer a delightful taste of history on your plate. Enjoy the simple pleasures and flavors reminiscent of a bygone era.

13. Wilted Lettuce Salad

Step into the pages of "The Grapes of Wrath" by John Steinbeck with this rustic and hearty Wilted Lettuce Salad. Inspired by the struggles and triumphs of the Joad family, this simple yet flavorful dish captures the essence of resilience and resourcefulness. The wilted lettuce reflects the harsh conditions faced by the characters, while the vibrant flavors speak to the hope and strength that persisted during their journey.

Serving: 4 servings
Preparation Time: 15 minutes
Ready Time: 20 minutes

Ingredients:
- 1 head of fresh iceberg lettuce, torn into bite-sized pieces
- 4 slices of thick-cut bacon, diced
- 1 small red onion, thinly sliced
- 2 tablespoons white sugar
- 1/4 cup apple cider vinegar
- Salt and pepper to taste
- 1 teaspoon Dijon mustard
- 1/4 cup olive oil

Instructions:
1. In a large salad bowl, place the torn iceberg lettuce and set aside.
2. In a skillet over medium heat, cook the diced bacon until it becomes crispy. Remove the bacon from the skillet and place it on a paper towel to drain excess grease.
3. In the same skillet with the bacon drippings, add the thinly sliced red onion. Cook for 2-3 minutes until the onion softens.
4. Sprinkle sugar over the onions and stir until the sugar dissolves.
5. Pour in the apple cider vinegar and Dijon mustard. Stir well, allowing the mixture to come to a simmer.
6. Drizzle the warm dressing over the lettuce in the salad bowl, tossing gently to wilt the lettuce slightly.
7. Add the crispy bacon to the salad and toss again to combine.
8. Season with salt and pepper to taste and drizzle olive oil over the salad, tossing one final time.
9. Serve the Wilted Lettuce Salad immediately, embracing the contrast of warm and cool elements.

Nutrition Information:
(Per serving)
- Calories: 210
- Fat: 15g
- Saturated Fat: 3.5g
- Cholesterol: 15mg
- Sodium: 320mg
- Carbohydrates: 15g
- Fiber: 2g
- Sugar: 10g
- Protein: 5g

Note: Nutrition information is approximate and may vary based on specific ingredients and serving sizes.

14. Pickled Pig's Feet

In John Steinbeck's masterpiece, "The Grapes of Wrath," the Joad family embarks on a journey through the harsh landscapes of the Dust Bowl era. Inspired by the resilience and resourcefulness of the characters, we present a recipe rooted in the frugality and creativity of the time – Pickled Pig's Feet. This dish captures the essence of making the most of what's available, transforming humble ingredients into a flavorful and hearty delicacy.

Serving: 4 servings
Preparation Time: 20 minutes
Ready Time: 72 hours (pickling time)

Ingredients:
- 4 pig's feet, cleaned and split in half
- 2 cups white vinegar
- 1 cup water
- 1 cup apple cider vinegar
- 1/2 cup brown sugar
- 1 tablespoon salt
- 2 teaspoons whole black peppercorns
- 4 cloves garlic, peeled and smashed

- 2 bay leaves
- 1 teaspoon red pepper flakes (optional)
- 1 onion, thinly sliced
- Fresh parsley for garnish

Instructions:
1. Begin by thoroughly cleaning the pig's feet, ensuring any excess debris is removed.
2. In a large pot, combine white vinegar, water, apple cider vinegar, brown sugar, salt, black peppercorns, garlic, bay leaves, and red pepper flakes if you desire a bit of heat. Bring the mixture to a boil, stirring to dissolve the sugar and salt.
3. Once the mixture has reached a boil, add the cleaned pig's feet to the pot. Reduce the heat to low, cover, and simmer for 2 hours, or until the pig's feet are tender.
4. Allow the pig's feet to cool in the liquid for about 30 minutes, then transfer them to a large, sterilized glass jar. Add the sliced onion to the jar.
5. Strain the cooking liquid and pour it over the pig's feet and onions in the jar. Ensure the pig's feet are fully submerged. Let the mixture cool to room temperature.
6. Once cooled, cover the jar with a lid and refrigerate for at least 72 hours to allow the flavors to meld and intensify.
7. To serve, plate the pickled pig's feet, garnishing with fresh parsley. Enjoy the unique flavors that harken back to a time of resilience and endurance.

Nutrition Information:
Note: Nutritional values are approximate and may vary based on specific ingredients used.
- Calories per serving: 300
- Protein: 25g
- Carbohydrates: 10g
- Fat: 18g
- Fiber: 2g
Embrace the spirit of "The Grapes of Wrath" with this Pickled Pig's Feet recipe, a testament to the strength found in resourcefulness and the simple joys of sustenance during challenging times.

15. Oakie Oatmeal Porridge

As we journey through the pages of John Steinbeck's "The Grapes of Wrath," we encounter a multitude of emotions and a sense of resilience in the face of adversity. Inspired by the spirit of the characters, we bring you the "Oakie Oatmeal Porridge," a hearty and wholesome dish that embodies the strength and sustenance needed to persevere through challenging times.

Serving: 4 servings
Preparation Time: 10 minutes
Ready Time: 20 minutes

Ingredients:
- 1 cup old-fashioned rolled oats
- 2 cups water
- 1 cup milk (dairy or plant-based)
- 1/4 teaspoon salt
- 2 tablespoons brown sugar or maple syrup
- 1/2 teaspoon ground cinnamon
- 1/4 cup raisins
- 1/4 cup chopped nuts (walnuts, almonds, or pecans)
- Fresh fruit for garnish (sliced bananas, berries, or apples)

Instructions:
1. Combine Oats and Liquid:
In a medium-sized saucepan, bring water and milk to a gentle boil over medium heat. Stir in the rolled oats and salt.
2. Simmer and Sweeten:
Reduce the heat to low and let the oats simmer, stirring occasionally. Add brown sugar or maple syrup and ground cinnamon, adjusting sweetness and spice to your liking.
3. Incorporate Raisins and Nuts:
When the oats are almost cooked, add raisins and chopped nuts. Continue simmering until the oats reach your desired consistency, absorbing the flavors of the added ingredients.
4. Serve Hot:
Once the Oakie Oatmeal Porridge reaches a creamy and thick consistency, remove the saucepan from heat. Spoon the porridge into bowls and garnish with fresh fruit slices.

Nutrition Information:
Note: Nutritional values may vary based on specific ingredients used.
- Calories per serving: ~250
- Protein: 8g
- Carbohydrates: 45g
- Dietary Fiber: 6g
- Sugars: 16g
- Fat: 6g
- Saturated Fat: 1g
- Cholesterol: 5mg
- Sodium: 150mg
- Potassium: 300mg
Conclusion:
The Oakie Oatmeal Porridge is not just a nourishing dish but a tribute to the resilience and strength found in the pages of "The Grapes of Wrath." May this comforting meal provide sustenance and warmth as you embark on your culinary journey inspired by the powerful narrative of John Steinbeck's classic novel.

16. Grilled Corn on the Cob

In the heartland of America, where the dust rises with the winds of change, there's a simplicity to life that is mirrored in the sustenance of the people. Inspired by John Steinbeck's classic novel, "The Grapes of Wrath," we present a dish that embodies the essence of resilience and the celebration of the harvest season – Grilled Corn on the Cob. A dish as humble as the Joad family, yet rich in flavor, this recipe pays homage to the enduring spirit of those who find solace and strength in the simplest of pleasures.

Serving: 4 servings
Preparation Time: 15 minutes
Ready Time: 25 minutes

Ingredients:
- 4 ears of fresh corn on the cob, husks intact
- 1/4 cup unsalted butter, melted

- 2 tablespoons olive oil
- 1 teaspoon smoked paprika
- 1 teaspoon garlic powder
- Salt and pepper to taste
- Fresh parsley, chopped (for garnish)

Instructions:
1. Prepare the Corn:
- Peel back the husks of the corn without removing them. Remove the silk from the corn, then pull the husks back up.
2. Soak the Corn:
- Place the prepared corn in a large bowl of water, ensuring they are fully submerged. Soak for at least 10 minutes to prevent the husks from burning during grilling.
3. Preheat the Grill:
- Preheat your grill to medium-high heat.
4. Season the Corn:
- In a small bowl, mix the melted butter, olive oil, smoked paprika, garlic powder, salt, and pepper.
5. Brush with Seasoning:
- Brush the seasoned mixture evenly over each ear of corn, ensuring they are well-coated.
6. Grill the Corn:
- Place the corn on the preheated grill, directly over the heat. Close the grill lid and cook for about 15 minutes, turning occasionally, until the husks are charred, and the corn is tender.
7. Garnish and Serve:
- Remove the corn from the grill, peel back the husks, and garnish with chopped fresh parsley. Serve immediately.

Nutrition Information:
(Per serving)
- Calories: 220
- Total Fat: 15g
- Saturated Fat: 7g
- Trans Fat: 0g
- Cholesterol: 30mg
- Sodium: 150mg
- Total Carbohydrates: 22g
- Dietary Fiber: 3g

- Sugars: 5g
- Protein: 3g

Embrace the flavors of the heartland with this simple yet soul-nourishing Grilled Corn on the Cob. As the Joads found strength in family, find comfort in every bite of this classic dish, honoring the enduring spirit of the land and its people.

17. Baked Apple Dumplings

Step into the world of John Steinbeck's "The Grapes of Wrath" with a culinary journey inspired by the flavors of the Dust Bowl era. One dish that captures the essence of resilience and simplicity is the Baked Apple Dumplings. These delightful treats encapsulate the warmth and comfort found amidst the challenges faced by the Joad family. So, let's embark on a culinary adventure that intertwines literature and the joy of good food.

Serving: 4 servings
Preparation Time: 20 minutes
Ready Time: 1 hour 15 minutes

Ingredients:
- 4 medium-sized apples (such as Granny Smith or Honeycrisp)
- 1/2 cup granulated sugar
- 1 teaspoon ground cinnamon
- 1/4 teaspoon ground nutmeg
- 1/4 cup unsalted butter, cut into small cubes
- 1 package refrigerated crescent roll dough
- 1/2 cup brown sugar, packed
- 1/2 cup water
- 1/2 teaspoon vanilla extract

Instructions:
1. Preheat your oven to 350°F (175°C).
2. Peel and core the apples, leaving the bottom intact. This creates a well for the filling.
3. In a small bowl, combine the granulated sugar, cinnamon, and nutmeg. Mix well.

4. Stuff each apple with the sugar and spice mixture, dividing it evenly among the apples. Top each apple with a few cubes of butter.
5. Unroll the crescent roll dough and separate it into triangles. Place an apple in the center of each triangle.
6. Wrap the dough around each apple, sealing the edges. Place the wrapped apples in a baking dish.
7. In a small saucepan, combine the brown sugar, water, and vanilla extract. Heat over medium heat, stirring until the sugar is dissolved. Pour this mixture over the wrapped apples.
8. Bake in the preheated oven for 45-50 minutes or until the dumplings are golden brown and the apples are tender.
9. Serve the baked apple dumplings warm, drizzled with the caramel sauce from the baking dish.

Nutrition Information:
(Per serving)
- Calories: 320 kcal
- Total Fat: 12g
- Saturated Fat: 7g
- Cholesterol: 30mg
- Sodium: 360mg
- Total Carbohydrates: 53g
- Dietary Fiber: 3g
- Sugars: 39g
- Protein: 1g
Indulge in the flavors of history and literature with these Baked Apple Dumplings, a tribute to the enduring spirit found within the pages of "The Grapes of Wrath."

18. Dust Storm Muffins

Step back in time to the Dust Bowl era with these Dust Storm Muffins, inspired by the hardships faced by the Joad family in John Steinbeck's iconic novel, "The Grapes of Wrath." These muffins capture the essence of survival and resilience, offering a blend of hearty ingredients that were common during the challenging times of the Great Depression. Enjoy the rustic flavors that tell a tale of endurance and strength.

Serving: 12 muffins
Preparation time: 15 minutes
Ready time: 30 minutes

Ingredients:
- 2 cups all-purpose flour
- 1 cup rolled oats
- 1/2 cup brown sugar, packed
- 1 tablespoon baking powder
- 1/2 teaspoon baking soda
- 1/2 teaspoon salt
- 1 teaspoon ground cinnamon
- 1/2 cup unsalted butter, melted
- 2 large eggs
- 1 cup milk
- 1 teaspoon vanilla extract
- 1 cup grated carrot
- 1/2 cup raisins
- 1/2 cup chopped walnuts

Instructions:
1. Preheat the oven to 375°F (190°C). Grease a muffin tin or line it with paper liners.
2. In a large bowl, combine the flour, rolled oats, brown sugar, baking powder, baking soda, salt, and ground cinnamon.
3. In a separate bowl, whisk together the melted butter, eggs, milk, and vanilla extract.
4. Pour the wet ingredients into the dry ingredients and stir until just combined. Do not overmix.
5. Fold in the grated carrot, raisins, and chopped walnuts until evenly distributed throughout the batter.
6. Spoon the batter into the prepared muffin tin, filling each cup about two-thirds full.
7. Bake in the preheated oven for 18-20 minutes or until a toothpick inserted into the center of a muffin comes out clean.
8. Allow the muffins to cool in the tin for 5 minutes before transferring them to a wire rack to cool completely.

Nutrition Information (per serving):
- Calories: 240

- Total Fat: 11g
- Saturated Fat: 5g
- Cholesterol: 50mg
- Sodium: 270mg
- Total Carbohydrates: 32g
- Dietary Fiber: 2g
- Sugars: 12g
- Protein: 5g

Note: Nutrition information is approximate and may vary based on specific ingredients used. Adjustments can be made for dietary preferences or restrictions.

19. Depression-Era Donuts

During the challenging times of the Great Depression, families struggled to make ends meet, inspiring resourcefulness and creativity in the kitchen. "Depression-Era Donuts" pays homage to the resilience and ingenuity of those difficult days, drawing inspiration from John Steinbeck's masterpiece, "The Grapes of Wrath." These simple yet delicious donuts are a testament to the power of simplicity and the ability to find joy in the midst of hardship.

Serving: Makes approximately 12 donuts.
Preparation Time: 15 minutes
Ready Time: 30 minutes

Ingredients:
- 2 cups all-purpose flour
- 1/2 cup sugar
- 1 tablespoon baking powder
- 1/2 teaspoon salt
- 1/2 teaspoon ground cinnamon
- 1/4 teaspoon ground nutmeg
- 1/2 cup milk
- 2 large eggs
- 2 tablespoons unsalted butter, melted
- 1 teaspoon vanilla extract
- Vegetable oil, for frying

Instructions:
1. In a large mixing bowl, whisk together the flour, sugar, baking powder, salt, cinnamon, and nutmeg.
2. In a separate bowl, combine the milk, eggs, melted butter, and vanilla extract. Mix well.
3. Pour the wet ingredients into the dry ingredients and stir until just combined. Be careful not to overmix; a few lumps are okay.
4. Heat vegetable oil in a large, deep skillet or pot to 350°F (175°C).
5. Using a tablespoon or a cookie scoop, drop spoonfuls of batter into the hot oil, frying 3-4 donuts at a time. Cook for 2-3 minutes on each side or until golden brown.
6. Remove the donuts with a slotted spoon and place them on a plate lined with paper towels to absorb excess oil.
7. Optional: While the donuts are still warm, roll them in a mixture of sugar and cinnamon for extra sweetness.
8. Allow the donuts to cool slightly before serving.

Nutrition Information:
(Per Serving)
- Calories: 150
- Total Fat: 6g
- Saturated Fat: 2.5g
- Cholesterol: 35mg
- Sodium: 180mg
- Total Carbohydrates: 21g
- Dietary Fiber: 1g
- Sugars: 8g
- Protein: 3g

These Depression-Era Donuts offer a taste of nostalgia and a glimpse into the resilience of families during a challenging chapter in history. Enjoy them with a cup of coffee and savor the simplicity and warmth that emanates from every bite.

20. Fruit Box Surprise

Delve into the heartland flavors of John Steinbeck's iconic novel, "The Grapes of Wrath," with our delightful creation, the "Fruit Box Surprise."

Inspired by the resilience and resourcefulness of the Joad family, this dish encapsulates the spirit of making the best out of what's available. Just like the Joads, who faced adversity with determination, our Fruit Box Surprise combines a medley of fruits to create a refreshing and satisfying treat that celebrates the abundance of the land.

Serving: 4 servings
Preparation Time: 15 minutes
Ready Time: 30 minutes

Ingredients:
- 2 apples, diced
- 2 pears, diced
- 1 cup grapes, halved
- 1 cup strawberries, sliced
- 1 cup pineapple chunks
- 1 cup watermelon, cubed
- 1 cup cantaloupe, cubed
- 1/2 cup honey or maple syrup
- 1 tablespoon fresh mint leaves, chopped (for garnish)

Instructions:
1. Prepare the Fruits:
- Wash and peel the apples and pears. Dice them into bite-sized pieces.
- Halve the grapes and slice the strawberries.
- Cube the watermelon and cantaloupe into small, uniform pieces.
2. Mix the Fruits:
- In a large mixing bowl, combine all the prepared fruits. Gently toss them together to create a colorful and vibrant fruit mix.
3. Sweeten the Surprise:
- Drizzle honey or maple syrup over the mixed fruits. Use more or less according to your sweetness preference.
4. Chill and Infuse:
- Place the fruit mixture in the refrigerator for at least 15 minutes to allow the flavors to meld and the fruits to chill.
5. Serve with a Twist:
- Before serving, garnish the Fruit Box Surprise with freshly chopped mint leaves for a burst of freshness.

Nutrition Information:

Note: Nutritional values may vary based on specific ingredients used and serving sizes.
- Calories: 150 per serving
- Total Fat: 0.5g
- Saturated Fat: 0g
- Trans Fat: 0g
- Cholesterol: 0mg
- Sodium: 5mg
- Total Carbohydrates: 38g
- Dietary Fiber: 4g
- Sugars: 28g
- Protein: 1g

Embrace the spirit of The Grapes of Wrath with this Fruit Box Surprise—a celebration of nature's bounty that mirrors the resilience and richness of the Joad family's journey. Perfect for a refreshing snack or a vibrant dessert, it captures the essence of making the most out of what the land provides.

21. Farmhouse Frittata

In "The Grapes of Wrath," John Steinbeck paints a vivid picture of the resilience and strength of the human spirit amidst adversity. Inspired by the themes of resilience and the importance of home, the Farmhouse Frittata captures the essence of hearty, simple meals found on the farms during the Great Depression era. This dish combines fresh ingredients commonly available on farms, creating a nourishing and flavorful meal that embodies the spirit of endurance and resourcefulness.

Serving: Serves 4-6 people
Preparation Time: 15 minutes
Ready Time: 35 minutes

Ingredients:
- 8 large eggs
- 1/4 cup milk
- 1 cup diced potatoes
- 1 cup diced bell peppers (assorted colors)
- 1 cup diced onions

- 1 cup diced tomatoes
- 1 cup chopped spinach or kale
- 1 cup grated cheddar cheese
- 2 tablespoons olive oil
- Salt and pepper to taste
- Fresh herbs (parsley or chives) for garnish (optional)

Instructions:
1. Preheat your oven to 375°F (190°C).
2. In a large bowl, whisk together the eggs and milk. Season with salt and pepper. Set aside.
3. Heat olive oil in a large oven-safe skillet over medium heat. Add diced potatoes and cook until they start to soften, about 5-6 minutes.
4. Add diced onions and bell peppers to the skillet. Sauté until the vegetables are tender, about 4-5 minutes.
5. Stir in the diced tomatoes and chopped spinach or kale. Cook for an additional 2-3 minutes until the spinach/kale wilts.
6. Spread the vegetable mixture evenly in the skillet. Pour the egg mixture over the vegetables, allowing it to cover the entire surface.
7. Cook on the stovetop for 2-3 minutes until the edges start to set.
8. Sprinkle grated cheddar cheese evenly over the top of the frittata.
9. Transfer the skillet to the preheated oven and bake for 15-20 minutes or until the eggs are set and the top is lightly golden.
10. Remove the frittata from the oven and let it cool for a few minutes. Garnish with fresh herbs if desired.
11. Slice the frittata into wedges and serve warm.

Nutrition Information (approximate values per serving, based on 4 servings):
- Calories: 290
- Total Fat: 18g
- Saturated Fat: 7g
- Cholesterol: 380mg
- Sodium: 340mg
- Total Carbohydrate: 15g
- Dietary Fiber: 3g
- Sugars: 5g
- Protein: 18g
Note: Nutrition information may vary based on specific ingredients used and serving sizes.

22. Vineyard Vinaigrette

Inspired by the agrarian setting and the simple, flavorful ingredients found in John Steinbeck's "The Grapes of Wrath," the Vineyard Vinaigrette captures the essence of bountiful harvests and the rustic charm of vineyards. This tangy dressing blends the robust flavors of grapes and herbs, evoking the essence of the land and the resilience of its people.

Serving: Makes approximately 1 cup of dressing.
Preparation time: 10 minutes
Ready time: 10 minutes

Ingredients:
- 1/2 cup seedless red grapes, halved
- 2 tablespoons red wine vinegar
- 1 tablespoon balsamic vinegar
- 1 teaspoon Dijon mustard
- 1 small shallot, finely chopped
- 1/4 cup extra-virgin olive oil
- Salt and freshly ground black pepper to taste
- 1 tablespoon fresh thyme leaves, chopped
- 1 teaspoon honey (optional, for added sweetness)

Instructions:
1. Prepare the Grapes: In a small bowl, gently crush half of the red grapes using a fork or potato masher to release their juices. Leave the other half intact for texture.
2. Make the Vinaigrette Base: In a separate mixing bowl, whisk together the red wine vinegar, balsamic vinegar, Dijon mustard, and shallot until well combined.
3. Combine Ingredients: Slowly drizzle in the olive oil while whisking continuously to emulsify the dressing. Add the crushed grapes and the whole grape halves to the mixture.
4. Season and Flavor: Season the vinaigrette with salt, freshly ground black pepper, and fresh thyme leaves. If desired, add a teaspoon of honey for a touch of sweetness.

5. Blend and Refrigerate: Whisk or shake the vinaigrette vigorously until all ingredients are well combined. For the best flavor, allow the vinaigrette to sit in the refrigerator for at least 30 minutes before serving to let the flavors meld together.

6. Serve: Drizzle this Vineyard Vinaigrette over a crisp green salad, roasted vegetables, or use it as a marinade for grilled poultry or fish. Shake well before each use.

Nutrition Information: *(per serving - 2 tablespoons)*
- Calories: 80 kcal
- Total Fat: 7g
- Saturated Fat: 1g
- Sodium: 35mg
- Total Carbohydrates: 4g
- Sugars: 3g
- Protein: 0.5g

Note: Nutritional values are approximate and may vary based on specific ingredients used.

This Vineyard Vinaigrette embodies the essence of the agricultural abundance celebrated in "The Grapes of Wrath," offering a delightful harmony of flavors that accentuate a variety of dishes, echoing the resilience and spirit of the characters within Steinbeck's iconic novel.

23. Grape Harvest Gumbo

Inspired by the resilience and resourcefulness depicted in John Steinbeck's "The Grapes of Wrath," Grape Harvest Gumbo pays homage to the flavors of the land and the communal spirit of sharing during difficult times. This flavorful gumbo celebrates the essence of the grape harvest and the hearty, comforting meals that bring people together in the face of adversity.

Serving: Serves: 6-8
Preparation Time: 20 minutes
Ready Time: Total: 1 hour 30 minutes

Ingredients:
- 1/2 cup vegetable oil

- 1/2 cup all-purpose flour
- 1 large onion, diced
- 1 green bell pepper, diced
- 2 celery stalks, diced
- 4 cloves garlic, minced
- 1 pound andouille sausage, sliced
- 1 pound chicken thighs, boneless and skinless, cut into cubes
- 6 cups chicken broth
- 1 can (14.5 oz) diced tomatoes, drained
- 1 cup okra, sliced
- 1 cup fresh or frozen sliced okra
- 1 cup fresh or frozen sliced okra
- 1 teaspoon dried thyme
- 1 teaspoon paprika
- 1/2 teaspoon cayenne pepper (adjust to taste)
- Salt and black pepper to taste
- 2 cups fresh grapes, halved and seeded
- 4 cups cooked white rice, for serving
- Chopped green onions, for garnish

Instructions:
1. In a large pot or Dutch oven, heat the vegetable oil over medium heat. Gradually whisk in the flour to create a roux, stirring constantly for about 20-25 minutes until the roux turns a deep brown color.
2. Add the diced onion, bell pepper, celery, and minced garlic to the roux. Cook, stirring occasionally, for about 5 minutes until the vegetables begin to soften.
3. Incorporate the andouille sausage slices and cubed chicken thighs into the pot, stirring occasionally until the chicken is no longer pink, about 7-8 minutes.
4. Pour in the chicken broth and diced tomatoes, stirring well to combine. Add the sliced okra, dried thyme, paprika, cayenne pepper, salt, and black pepper. Bring the mixture to a boil.
5. Reduce the heat to low and let the gumbo simmer, uncovered, for approximately 45 minutes to an hour, allowing the flavors to meld and the gumbo to thicken. Stir occasionally.
6. Once the gumbo has thickened to your desired consistency, add the halved grapes and cook for an additional 5 minutes until the grapes are warmed through.
7. Adjust seasoning if needed and remove the pot from heat.

8. Serve the Grape Harvest Gumbo over cooked white rice, garnished with chopped green onions.

Nutrition Information:
(*Note: Nutritional values are approximate and may vary based on ingredients used*)
- Calories: 450 kcal
- Total Fat: 25g
- Saturated Fat: 7g
- Trans Fat: 0g
- Cholesterol: 85mg
- Sodium: 1150mg
- Total Carbohydrates: 32g
- Dietary Fiber: 4g
- Sugars: 8g
- Protein: 25g

This Grape Harvest Gumbo is a delightful blend of savory and sweet flavors, offering a taste of warmth and togetherness reminiscent of the strength found within the pages of "The Grapes of Wrath." Enjoy this nourishing dish that pays homage to the enduring human spirit in challenging times.

24. Fruit Box Stew

Step into the world of The Grapes of Wrath with this hearty and wholesome "Fruit Box Stew." Inspired by the resilience of the Joad family as they journeyed through the Dust Bowl, this dish captures the essence of resourcefulness and simplicity. The Fruit Box Stew pays homage to the era's scarcity by turning basic ingredients into a nourishing and flavorful meal that transcends hardship. So, let's embark on a culinary journey reminiscent of the Joads' indomitable spirit with this delicious and easy-to-make stew.

Serving: 4 servings
Preparation Time: 15 minutes
Ready Time: 45 minutes

Ingredients:

- 2 tablespoons olive oil
- 1 onion, diced
- 2 cloves garlic, minced
- 4 carrots, peeled and sliced
- 4 potatoes, peeled and diced
- 2 apples, cored and chopped
- 1 can (15 oz) diced tomatoes
- 1 can (15 oz) black beans, drained and rinsed
- 4 cups vegetable broth
- 1 teaspoon dried thyme
- 1 teaspoon dried rosemary
- Salt and pepper to taste

Instructions:
1. In a large pot, heat the olive oil over medium heat. Add diced onions and minced garlic, sautéing until onions are translucent.
2. Add sliced carrots and diced potatoes to the pot, stirring occasionally until they begin to soften.
3. Incorporate chopped apples, diced tomatoes, and black beans into the pot. Mix well to combine the flavors.
4. Pour in the vegetable broth, and add dried thyme and rosemary. Season with salt and pepper to taste. Bring the stew to a gentle boil.
5. Reduce heat to low, cover the pot, and let the stew simmer for approximately 30 minutes, allowing the flavors to meld and the vegetables to become tender.
6. Taste and adjust seasoning if necessary. Serve the Fruit Box Stew hot, allowing its comforting aroma to transport you to the heart of The Grapes of Wrath.

Nutrition Information (per serving):
- Calories: 320
- Protein: 8g
- Carbohydrates: 58g
- Fiber: 12g
- Sugars: 12g
- Fat: 8g
- Saturated Fat: 1g
- Cholesterol: 0mg
- Sodium: 800mg

Note: Nutrition information is approximate and may vary based on specific ingredients used.

25. Oakie Onion Rings

Inspired by the indomitable spirit and resourcefulness depicted in John Steinbeck's "The Grapes of Wrath," Oakie Onion Rings pay homage to the resilience of the Oakies. These crispy, golden rings represent the simplicity and sustenance sought by the Joad family and their fellow travelers during the Great Depression. Easy to prepare yet rich in flavor, these onion rings evoke a sense of comfort and nostalgia.

Serving: 4 servings
Preparation time: 15 minutes
Ready time: 25 minutes

Ingredients:
- 2 large yellow onions, sliced into rings
- 1 cup all-purpose flour
- 1 teaspoon garlic powder
- 1 teaspoon paprika
- 1 teaspoon salt
- 1/2 teaspoon black pepper
- 1 cup buttermilk
- Vegetable oil, for frying

Instructions:
1. Peel the onions and slice them into rings about 1/2 inch thick. Separate the rings and set them aside.
2. In a shallow bowl, combine the flour, garlic powder, paprika, salt, and black pepper. Mix well to create the seasoned flour.
3. Pour the buttermilk into another shallow bowl.
4. Heat vegetable oil in a deep skillet or frying pan over medium-high heat until it reaches 350°F (175°C).
5. Dip the onion rings into the seasoned flour, ensuring they are evenly coated. Shake off any excess flour.
6. Next, dip the floured rings into the buttermilk, allowing any excess to drip off.

7. Dip the rings back into the seasoned flour for a second coating, ensuring they are fully coated.
8. Carefully place the coated onion rings into the hot oil, a few at a time, without overcrowding the pan.
9. Fry the rings for 2-3 minutes per side, or until they turn golden brown and crispy. Use tongs to flip them halfway through the cooking process.
10. Once golden and crispy, remove the onion rings from the oil and place them on a paper towel-lined plate to drain excess oil.
11. Repeat the frying process with the remaining onion rings.

Nutrition Information (per serving):
Please note that Nutrition Information is approximate and may vary based on ingredients and cooking methods used.
- Calories: 240
- Total Fat: 8g
- Saturated Fat: 1g
- Cholesterol: 3mg
- Sodium: 590mg
- Total Carbohydrate: 37g
- Dietary Fiber: 3g
- Sugars: 6g
- Protein: 5g
Enjoy these Oakie Onion Rings as a nostalgic side dish or a delightful snack, celebrating the enduring spirit found within the pages of "The Grapes of Wrath."

26. Bankrupt Banana Bread

In the spirit of resilience and resourcefulness depicted in John Steinbeck's "The Grapes of Wrath," where characters faced adversity with determination, we present the "Bankrupt Banana Bread" recipe. This thrifty and delicious banana bread is a nod to making the most of limited resources, much like the characters in the novel.

Serving: Makes 1 loaf (about 10 slices)
Preparation Time: 15 minutes
Ready Time: 1 hour 15 minutes

Ingredients:
- 3 ripe bananas, mashed
- 1/2 cup vegetable oil
- 1 cup sugar
- 2 large eggs
- 1 teaspoon vanilla extract
- 1 1/2 cups all-purpose flour
- 1 teaspoon baking soda
- 1/2 teaspoon baking powder
- 1/2 teaspoon salt
- 1/2 teaspoon ground cinnamon
- 1/4 teaspoon ground nutmeg
- 1/4 cup milk
- 1/2 cup chopped nuts (optional)

Instructions:
1. Preheat your oven to 350°F (175°C). Grease and flour a 9x5-inch loaf pan.
2. In a large mixing bowl, combine mashed bananas, vegetable oil, sugar, eggs, and vanilla extract. Mix well until the ingredients are fully incorporated.
3. In a separate bowl, whisk together the flour, baking soda, baking powder, salt, cinnamon, and nutmeg.
4. Gradually add the dry ingredients to the banana mixture, stirring until just combined.
5. Pour in the milk and continue to mix until the batter is smooth. If desired, fold in chopped nuts.
6. Pour the batter into the prepared loaf pan, spreading it evenly.
7. Bake in the preheated oven for 60-70 minutes or until a toothpick inserted into the center comes out clean.
8. Allow the banana bread to cool in the pan for 10 minutes before transferring it to a wire rack to cool completely.

Nutrition Information:
Per Serving (1 slice):
- Calories: 220
- Total Fat: 10g
- Saturated Fat: 1.5g
- Trans Fat: 0g
- Cholesterol: 30mg

- Sodium: 180mg
- Total Carbohydrates: 31g
- Dietary Fiber: 2g
- Sugars: 16g
- Protein: 3g

Note: Nutrition information is approximate and may vary based on specific ingredients used.

27. Boxcar Banana Pudding

Embark on a culinary journey through the Dust Bowl era with the "Boxcar Banana Pudding," inspired by John Steinbeck's timeless classic, "The Grapes of Wrath." This hearty and comforting dessert pays homage to the resourcefulness and resilience of those who endured challenging times. Just like the characters in the novel, this pudding is a simple yet satisfying treat that brings warmth and sweetness to the table.

Serving: 6-8 servings
Preparation Time: 20 minutes
Ready Time: 4 hours (includes chilling time)

Ingredients:
- 4 ripe bananas, sliced
- 1 box of vanilla wafers
- 2 1/2 cups whole milk
- 3/4 cup granulated sugar
- 1/3 cup all-purpose flour
- 1/4 teaspoon salt
- 4 large egg yolks, beaten
- 2 teaspoons pure vanilla extract
- 1 cup heavy cream
- 2 tablespoons powdered sugar
- Optional: banana slices and crushed vanilla wafers for garnish

Instructions:
1. In a medium saucepan, combine the sugar, flour, and salt. Gradually whisk in the milk until smooth.

2. Cook the mixture over medium heat, stirring constantly, until it thickens and comes to a boil. This should take about 8-10 minutes.
3. Once the mixture has thickened, remove it from the heat. In a separate bowl, whisk the egg yolks. Gradually whisk in about 1 cup of the hot milk mixture to temper the eggs.
4. Pour the egg mixture back into the saucepan with the remaining hot milk mixture, whisking constantly to prevent the eggs from curdling.
5. Return the saucepan to the heat and cook for an additional 2 minutes, or until the pudding has a custard-like consistency. Remove from heat and stir in the vanilla extract.
6. In a trifle dish or individual serving glasses, layer vanilla wafers, sliced bananas, and the warm pudding mixture. Repeat the layers until all ingredients are used, finishing with a layer of pudding on top.
7. Cover the pudding with plastic wrap, ensuring it touches the surface of the pudding to prevent a skin from forming. Chill in the refrigerator for at least 4 hours or overnight.
8. Before serving, whip the heavy cream and powdered sugar until stiff peaks form. Spread the whipped cream over the chilled pudding.
9. Optionally, garnish with banana slices and crushed vanilla wafers for a decorative touch.

Nutrition Information:
(Per serving - based on 8 servings)
- Calories: 380
- Total Fat: 19g
- Saturated Fat: 11g
- Cholesterol: 155mg
- Sodium: 170mg
- Total Carbohydrates: 48g
- Dietary Fiber: 2g
- Sugars: 31g
- Protein: 5g

Indulge in this Boxcar Banana Pudding, a delightful dessert that captures the essence of an era marked by hardships and tenacity. Each spoonful is a taste of history and a celebration of the human spirit.

28. Almond Orchard Albatross

Embark on a culinary journey inspired by John Steinbeck's masterpiece, "The Grapes of Wrath," with our delightful creation, the "Almond Orchard Albatross." This dish pays homage to the resilience of the Okies and their connection to the land, blending flavors that reflect the agricultural richness of the time.

Serving: 4 servings
Preparation Time: 20 minutes
Ready Time: 45 minutes

Ingredients:
- 4 boneless, skinless chicken breasts
- 1 cup almond meal
- 1/2 cup all-purpose flour
- 1 teaspoon salt
- 1/2 teaspoon black pepper
- 1/2 teaspoon smoked paprika
- 1/4 cup olive oil
- 1/2 cup white wine
- 1 cup chicken broth
- 1/2 cup heavy cream
- 1 cup sliced mushrooms
- 1/2 cup slivered almonds, toasted
- Fresh parsley, chopped (for garnish)

Instructions:
1. Preheat Oven:
Preheat your oven to 375°F (190°C).
2. Prepare Chicken:
a. In a shallow bowl, combine almond meal, all-purpose flour, salt, black pepper, and smoked paprika.
b. Dredge each chicken breast in the almond-flour mixture, ensuring an even coating.
3. Sear Chicken:
Heat olive oil in an oven-safe skillet over medium-high heat. Sear the chicken breasts until golden brown on both sides.
4. Create Sauce:
a. Remove the chicken from the skillet and set aside.
b. Deglaze the skillet with white wine, scraping up any browned bits.
c. Add chicken broth and heavy cream, stirring until well combined.

5. Simmer and Bake:
a. Allow the sauce to simmer for 5 minutes, then return the seared chicken to the skillet.
b. Transfer the skillet to the preheated oven and bake for 25-30 minutes or until the chicken reaches an internal temperature of 165°F (74°C).
6. Saute Mushrooms:
In a separate pan, sauté sliced mushrooms until tender.
7. Assemble:
Arrange the baked chicken on a serving platter, spoon the creamy mushroom sauce over the top, and sprinkle with toasted slivered almonds.
8. Garnish:
Finish with a sprinkle of fresh chopped parsley for a burst of color and freshness.

Nutrition Information:
(Per Serving)
- Calories: 480
- Total Fat: 30g
- Saturated Fat: 10g
- Trans Fat: 0g
- Cholesterol: 120mg
- Sodium: 800mg
- Total Carbohydrates: 12g
- Dietary Fiber: 3g
- Sugars: 1g
- Protein: 40g
Delight in the "Almond Orchard Albatross," a dish that encapsulates the flavors of the era and the enduring spirit of those who braved the journey.

29. Cornfield Cassoulet

Step into the heartland of The Grapes of Wrath with a culinary journey inspired by the resilience and spirit of the Joad family. The Cornfield Cassoulet pays homage to the fields of plenty and the simple yet profound pleasures of a good meal. This hearty dish encapsulates the essence of sustenance in times of adversity, echoing the themes of Steinbeck's masterpiece.

Serving: Serves 6
Preparation Time: 20 minutes
Ready Time: 2 hours

Ingredients:
- 1 pound dried white beans, soaked overnight
- 4 cups corn kernels (fresh or frozen)
- 1 onion, finely chopped
- 3 cloves garlic, minced
- 2 carrots, diced
- 2 celery stalks, diced
- 1 red bell pepper, diced
- 1 green bell pepper, diced
- 1 can (14 ounces) diced tomatoes
- 1 cup vegetable broth
- 1 teaspoon dried thyme
- 1 teaspoon dried rosemary
- Salt and pepper to taste
- 1/4 cup olive oil
- 1 pound smoked sausage, sliced
- 1 cup breadcrumbs
- Fresh parsley for garnish

Instructions:
1. In a large pot, combine the soaked white beans and enough water to cover them. Bring to a boil and then simmer until the beans are tender (about 1 hour). Drain and set aside.
2. In a large, oven-safe Dutch oven, heat olive oil over medium heat. Add onions and garlic, sauté until fragrant.
3. Add carrots, celery, and bell peppers. Cook until the vegetables are softened.
4. Stir in corn, diced tomatoes, vegetable broth, thyme, rosemary, salt, and pepper. Bring to a simmer.
5. Preheat your oven to 350°F (175°C).
6. Add the cooked white beans and sliced smoked sausage to the vegetable mixture, combining everything evenly.
7. Sprinkle breadcrumbs over the top for a delightful crunch.

8. Cover the Dutch oven and transfer it to the preheated oven. Bake for 1 hour, allowing the flavors to meld and the breadcrumbs to turn golden.
9. Once done, remove from the oven and let it rest for a few minutes.
10. Garnish with fresh parsley before serving.

Nutrition Information:
Note: Nutrition information is approximate and may vary based on specific ingredients and serving sizes.
- Calories per serving: 450
- Total Fat: 18g
- Cholesterol: 30mg
- Sodium: 800mg
- Total Carbohydrates: 55g
- Dietary Fiber: 12g
- Sugars: 8g
- Protein: 20g

Indulge in the warmth of the Cornfield Cassoulet, a dish that brings the fields of plenty to your table, celebrating the enduring spirit of the human journey.

30. Oakie Orange Sorbet

In John Steinbeck's "The Grapes of Wrath," the Joad family endures hardship yet finds solace in simple pleasures and resourcefulness. Inspired by their resilience, the Oakie Orange Sorbet pays homage to the tenacity of the characters, offering a refreshing treat in challenging times. This zesty sorbet captures the essence of hope and rejuvenation amidst adversity.

Serving: Makes approximately 6 servings.
Preparation Time: 20 minutes
Ready Time: 4-6 hours (including freezing time)

Ingredients:
- 4 cups freshly squeezed orange juice (from about 8-10 oranges)
- Zest from 2 oranges
- 1 cup granulated sugar
- 1 cup water

- 2 tablespoons fresh lemon juice

Instructions:
1. Prepare the Orange Juice: Begin by juicing the oranges to yield approximately 4 cups of fresh orange juice. Ensure the juice is strained to remove any pulp or seeds. Zest two oranges and set the zest aside for later use.
2. Create the Simple Syrup: In a saucepan, combine the granulated sugar, water, and orange zest. Bring the mixture to a gentle boil over medium heat, stirring occasionally until the sugar completely dissolves. Simmer for 5 minutes to infuse the syrup with the orange zest flavor. Remove from heat and let it cool completely.
3. Combine Ingredients: In a mixing bowl, combine the freshly squeezed orange juice, strained simple syrup (once cooled), and fresh lemon juice. Stir well to ensure the ingredients are fully blended.
4. Chill the Mixture: Cover the mixing bowl and refrigerate the orange mixture for at least 2 hours, allowing the flavors to meld together thoroughly.
5. Freeze the Sorbet: Once the mixture is properly chilled, transfer it into an ice cream maker and churn according to the manufacturer's instructions until it reaches a sorbet consistency.
6. Final Freeze: Transfer the churned sorbet into a freezer-safe container, smoothing the top with a spatula. Cover the container with a lid or plastic wrap, and let it freeze for an additional 2-4 hours until firm.
7. Serve: When ready to serve, scoop the Oakie Orange Sorbet into bowls or dessert cups. Garnish with a twist of orange zest or a slice of fresh orange for an extra touch.

Nutrition Information (per serving, approximate):
- Calories: 160
- Total Fat: 0g
- Cholesterol: 0mg
- Sodium: 0mg
- Total Carbohydrates: 41g
- Dietary Fiber: 0.5g
- Sugars: 38g
- Protein: 1g
Note: Nutrition information may vary based on specific ingredients used and serving sizes.

This Oakie Orange Sorbet offers a delightful burst of citrusy freshness, embodying the resilience and hope found amidst challenging circumstances, much like the spirit depicted in "The Grapes of Wrath." Enjoy this refreshing treat as a tribute to perseverance and the simple pleasures in life.

31. Depression Dogs

'Depression Dogs" pays homage to the resilience and resourcefulness showcased in Steinbeck's "The Grapes of Wrath." These hot dogs symbolize the struggle and creativity during challenging times, combining simple ingredients into a flavorful dish that represents endurance and perseverance.

Serving: 4 servings
Preparation time: 10 minutes
Ready time: 20 minutes

Ingredients:
- 4 hot dog buns
- 4 hot dogs (beef, chicken, or vegetarian substitute)
- 1 onion, thinly sliced
- 1 tablespoon olive oil
- 1 teaspoon paprika
- 1 teaspoon garlic powder
- Salt and pepper to taste
- Mustard and ketchup for serving (optional)

Instructions:
1. Prepare the Onions: Heat olive oil in a skillet over medium heat. Add the thinly sliced onions and sauté until they become caramelized and golden brown, stirring occasionally. This process may take about 8-10 minutes.
2. Cook the Hot Dogs: While the onions are cooking, prepare the hot dogs. Grill, pan-fry, or boil them according to your preference until they're cooked through.
3. Season: Sprinkle the paprika, garlic powder, salt, and pepper over the caramelized onions. Stir to coat the onions evenly with the seasoning.

4. Assemble the Depression Dogs: Place the cooked hot dogs in the buns. Top each hot dog with a generous portion of the seasoned caramelized onions.

5. Serve: Optionally, serve with mustard and ketchup or any other condiments of your choice.

Nutrition Information (per serving, without condiments):
- Calories: 300
- Total Fat: 14g
- Saturated Fat: 4g
- Cholesterol: 30mg
- Sodium: 650mg
- Total Carbohydrate: 32g
- Dietary Fiber: 2g
- Sugars: 6g
- Protein: 12g

This dish captures the essence of making do with what's available, turning humble ingredients into a satisfying meal reminiscent of challenging times. Enjoy these Depression Dogs as a tribute to resilience in the face of adversity.

32. Migrant Minestrone

The Grapes of Wrath by John Steinbeck vividly portrays the struggles faced by migrant families during the Great Depression. The Migrant Minestrone, inspired by their resilience, pays homage to their journey. This hearty soup reflects resourcefulness, incorporating simple yet nourishing ingredients, symbolizing hope amidst adversity.

Serving: 6-8 servings
Preparation time: 15 minutes
Ready time: 45 minutes

Ingredients:
- 2 tablespoons olive oil
- 1 onion, diced
- 2 cloves garlic, minced
- 2 carrots, diced

- 2 celery stalks, diced
- 1 zucchini, diced
- 1 can (14 oz) diced tomatoes
- 1 can (14 oz) kidney beans, drained and rinsed
- 6 cups vegetable or chicken broth
- 1 teaspoon dried oregano
- 1 teaspoon dried basil
- Salt and pepper to taste
- 1 cup small pasta (such as ditalini or small shells)
- Grated Parmesan cheese (optional, for serving)

Instructions:
1. Heat olive oil in a large pot over medium heat. Add diced onions and sauté until translucent, about 3-4 minutes. Add minced garlic and cook for an additional minute.
2. Stir in diced carrots, celery, and zucchini. Cook for 5-7 minutes until the vegetables begin to soften.
3. Add the diced tomatoes (with their juices), kidney beans, broth, dried oregano, dried basil, salt, and pepper. Bring the soup to a boil.
4. Once boiling, reduce heat to a simmer and let it cook for 20-25 minutes, allowing the flavors to meld together.
5. Stir in the pasta and cook for another 10-12 minutes or until the pasta is tender but still firm to the bite.
6. Adjust seasoning if needed. Serve hot, optionally topped with grated Parmesan cheese.

Nutrition Information (per serving):
- Calories: 220
- Total Fat: 5g
- Saturated Fat: 1g
- Cholesterol: 0mg
- Sodium: 780mg
- Total Carbohydrate: 36g
- Dietary Fiber: 8g
- Sugars: 7g
- Protein: 9g

Note: Nutrition information is approximate and may vary based on specific ingredients used. Adjustments can be made based on dietary needs or preferences.

33. Barley Wine Brew

Step into the world of The Grapes of Wrath with a hearty and robust Barley Wine Brew. Inspired by the resilience of the Joad family, this rich and flavorful brew pays homage to the enduring spirit found within the pages of John Steinbeck's masterpiece. With a perfect blend of malt sweetness and hop bitterness, this Barley Wine Brew is sure to transport you to the dusty landscapes and heartfelt journeys of the Dust Bowl era.

Serving: Enjoy this Barley Wine Brew in a tulip glass at a cozy gathering with friends or as a contemplative sipper by the fireplace. It pairs exceptionally well with aged cheeses, roasted meats, or simply on its own as you reflect on the struggles and triumphs of the characters in The Grapes of Wrath.
Preparation Time: 30 minutes
Ready Time: 8-12 weeks (including fermentation and aging)

Ingredients:
- 10 lbs pale malt
- 1 lb caramel malt (60L)
- 1 lb Munich malt
- 0.5 lb biscuit malt
- 1 oz East Kent Goldings hops (60 minutes)
- 0.5 oz East Kent Goldings hops (30 minutes)
- 0.5 oz East Kent Goldings hops (15 minutes)
- 0.5 oz East Kent Goldings hops (5 minutes)
- 1 tsp Irish moss (15 minutes)
- 1 packet English ale yeast
- 1 cup priming sugar (for bottling)

Instructions:
1. Heat 3.5 gallons of water in your brew kettle to around 165°F (74°C). Add crushed grains to a grain bag and steep in the hot water for 30 minutes. Remove the grain bag and let it drain back into the kettle.
2. Bring the liquid (wort) to a boil and add the 60-minute hop addition. Boil for 30 minutes before adding the 30-minute hop addition.

3. After another 15 minutes, add the 15-minute hop addition and Irish moss. Continue boiling for an additional 10 minutes before adding the final 5-minute hop addition.

4. Cool the wort quickly using a wort chiller or an ice bath. Transfer the cooled wort to a sanitized fermenter.

5. Pitch the yeast into the fermenter and seal it with an airlock. Allow the beer to ferment at a controlled temperature around 65-70°F (18-21°C) for 2-3 weeks.

6. After primary fermentation, transfer the beer to a secondary fermenter for an additional 4-8 weeks for aging. This extended aging period is crucial for developing the complex flavors of a barley wine.

7. Bottle the beer with priming sugar and let it carbonate for at least 2 weeks before enjoying.

Nutrition Information (per 12 oz serving):
- Calories: 300
- Carbohydrates: 26g
- Protein: 2.5g
- Fat: 0g
- Alcohol by volume (ABV): 10%

34. Rutabaga Roulade

In the spirit of John Steinbeck's iconic novel, "The Grapes of Wrath," we present a hearty and humble dish inspired by the resilience of the Joad family. The Rutabaga Roulade pays homage to the simplicity and resourcefulness prevalent in the Dust Bowl era. This comforting dish transforms the often-overlooked rutabaga into a savory and satisfying centerpiece, symbolizing the strength and adaptability of those enduring challenging times.

Serving: 4-6 servings
Preparation Time: 20 minutes
Ready Time: 1 hour 30 minutes

Ingredients:
- 1 large rutabaga, peeled and thinly sliced lengthwise
- 2 tablespoons olive oil

- 1 onion, finely chopped
- 2 cloves garlic, minced
- 1 cup spinach, chopped
- 1 cup mushrooms, finely diced
- Salt and pepper to taste
- 1 cup ricotta cheese
- 1/2 cup grated Parmesan cheese
- 1 teaspoon dried thyme
- 1 teaspoon dried oregano
- 1 cup marinara sauce
- Fresh parsley for garnish

Instructions:
1. Preheat Oven:
Preheat your oven to 375°F (190°C).
2. Prepare Rutabaga Slices:
- Peel the rutabaga and slice it lengthwise into thin, uniform slices.
- Brush the slices lightly with olive oil and season with salt and pepper.
- Roast the rutabaga slices in the oven for 15-20 minutes until they become pliable.
3. Prepare Filling:
- In a skillet, heat olive oil over medium heat. Add chopped onions and garlic, sauté until translucent.
- Add mushrooms and spinach to the skillet, cooking until the vegetables are tender.
- Season with salt and pepper, thyme, and oregano. Remove from heat.
4. Prepare Cheese Mixture:
- In a bowl, combine ricotta and Parmesan cheese. Mix well.
5. Assemble Roulade:
- Lay out the roasted rutabaga slices.
- Spread the cheese mixture evenly over each slice.
- Spoon the vegetable mixture on top of the cheese layer.
- Carefully roll the rutabaga slices to form a roulade.
6. Bake:
- Place the rutabaga roulades in a baking dish.
- Pour marinara sauce over the top.
- Bake in the oven for 30-40 minutes until the roulades are golden and bubbly.
7. Garnish and Serve:
- Remove from the oven and let it rest for a few minutes.

- Garnish with fresh parsley.
- Slice and serve warm, accompanied by additional marinara sauce if desired.

Nutrition Information:
(Per Serving)
- Calories: 280
- Protein: 12g
- Fat: 15g
- Carbohydrates: 25g
- Fiber: 7g
- Sugars: 8g

This Rutabaga Roulade is a nourishing and flavorful tribute to the enduring spirit depicted in "The Grapes of Wrath." Enjoy this comforting dish with family and friends as you reflect on the strength and resilience of the human spirit during challenging times.

35. Labor Camp Lentils

As we journey through the pages of John Steinbeck's timeless classic, "The Grapes of Wrath," we encounter a vivid portrayal of hardship and resilience during the Dust Bowl era. In the spirit of the novel's indomitable spirit, we present "Labor Camp Lentils" — a humble yet hearty dish inspired by the endurance of those facing adversity. This recipe pays homage to the strength found in the most basic of ingredients, echoing the resourcefulness and determination of the characters in Steinbeck's masterpiece.

Serving: 4-6 servings
Preparation Time: 15 minutes
Ready Time: 1 hour

Ingredients:
- 1 cup dried lentils, rinsed and drained
- 1 onion, finely chopped
- 2 carrots, diced
- 2 celery stalks, finely chopped
- 3 cloves garlic, minced

- 1 can (14 oz) diced tomatoes
- 4 cups vegetable broth
- 1 teaspoon ground cumin
- 1 teaspoon smoked paprika
- 1/2 teaspoon dried thyme
- Salt and pepper to taste
- 2 tablespoons olive oil
- Fresh parsley for garnish (optional)

Instructions:
1. Heat olive oil in a large pot over medium heat. Add chopped onions, carrots, and celery. Sauté until the vegetables are softened, about 5 minutes.
2. Add minced garlic to the pot and sauté for an additional 1-2 minutes until fragrant.
3. Stir in the dried lentils, diced tomatoes, vegetable broth, ground cumin, smoked paprika, dried thyme, salt, and pepper.
4. Bring the mixture to a boil, then reduce the heat to low. Cover the pot and simmer for 45-50 minutes, or until the lentils are tender.
5. Once the lentils are cooked, taste and adjust the seasoning if needed. If you prefer a thicker consistency, you can mash some of the lentils with the back of a spoon.
6. Ladle the Labor Camp Lentils into bowls, garnish with fresh parsley if desired, and serve hot.

Nutrition Information:
(Per serving, based on 6 servings)
- Calories: 230
- Protein: 14g
- Fat: 4g
- Carbohydrates: 38g
- Fiber: 15g
- Sugar: 6g
- Sodium: 780mg

Embrace the simplicity and fortitude of "Labor Camp Lentils" as you share a meal that echoes the resilience found within the pages of "The Grapes of Wrath."

36. Vintage Vinegar Slaw

In John Steinbeck's "The Grapes of Wrath," food embodies resilience and adaptation during challenging times. Inspired by this tale of endurance, the Vintage Vinegar Slaw captures the essence of resourcefulness with its simple yet flavorsome ingredients. This tangy slaw pays homage to the spirit of making the most of what's available, much like the Joad family did on their journey.

Serving: 6 servings
Preparation time: 15 minutes
Ready time: 30 minutes

Ingredients:
- 1 medium head green cabbage, shredded
- 2 large carrots, grated
- 1 small onion, thinly sliced
- 1/2 cup apple cider vinegar
- 1/4 cup olive oil
- 2 tablespoons honey
- 1 teaspoon Dijon mustard
- Salt and pepper to taste
- Chopped parsley for garnish (optional)

Instructions:
1. In a large bowl, combine the shredded cabbage, grated carrots, and sliced onion.
2. In a separate bowl, whisk together the apple cider vinegar, olive oil, honey, Dijon mustard, salt, and pepper until well combined.
3. Pour the dressing over the cabbage mixture and toss until the vegetables are evenly coated.
4. Cover the slaw and refrigerate for at least 15 minutes to allow the flavors to meld.
5. Before serving, give the slaw a final toss and adjust seasoning if needed. Garnish with chopped parsley if desired.

Nutrition Information (per serving):
- Calories: 120
- Total Fat: 7g
- Saturated Fat: 1g

- Cholesterol: 0mg
- Sodium: 70mg
- Total Carbohydrate: 14g
- Dietary Fiber: 4g
- Sugars: 8g
- Protein: 2g

This Vintage Vinegar Slaw offers a crisp, refreshing bite with a delightful tang. It's a versatile side dish that pairs wonderfully with hearty mains or as a topping for sandwiches, embodying the resilience and adaptability celebrated in Steinbeck's masterpiece.

37. Tractor Tire Tacos

In "The Grapes of Wrath," the Joad family's journey symbolizes resilience in the face of hardship, much like these Tractor Tire Tacos. With a nod to the ruggedness of the road and the ingenuity of making do with what's available, these hearty tacos celebrate resourcefulness and flavor in every bite.

Serving: 4-6 servings
Preparation time: 20 minutes
Ready time: 40 minutes

Ingredients:
- 1 pound ground beef or alternative (e.g., lentils for a vegetarian option)
- 1 onion, diced
- 2 cloves garlic, minced
- 1 teaspoon chili powder
- 1 teaspoon ground cumin
- 1 teaspoon paprika
- Salt and pepper to taste
- 1 can (14 ounces) black beans, drained and rinsed
- 1 can (14 ounces) diced tomatoes
- 1 cup corn kernels
- 12-15 small corn or flour tortillas
- 1 cup shredded cheese (cheddar or Monterey Jack)
- Optional toppings: diced tomatoes, shredded lettuce, sliced jalapeños, sour cream, avocado slices, salsa

Instructions:
1. Heat a skillet over medium heat. Add the ground beef (or alternative) and cook until browned, breaking it into crumbles. Drain excess fat if needed.
2. Add diced onions and minced garlic to the skillet. Sauté until the onions are translucent.
3. Stir in the chili powder, ground cumin, paprika, salt, and pepper. Cook for another 2 minutes to allow the spices to bloom.
4. Add the black beans, diced tomatoes, and corn kernels to the skillet. Mix well and let it simmer for 10-15 minutes, allowing the flavors to meld together. Adjust seasoning if needed.
5. While the filling simmers, preheat the oven to 350°F (175°C). Warm the tortillas in the oven for 5-7 minutes, until they are pliable.
6. Assemble the tacos by spooning the filling onto each warmed tortilla. Top with shredded cheese and any desired toppings.
7. Serve the Tractor Tire Tacos hot and enjoy this flavorful homage to resilience on a plate!

Nutrition Information:
(Per serving, assuming 4 servings)
Calories: 550
Total Fat: 20g
Saturated Fat: 8g
Cholesterol: 80mg
Sodium: 800mg
Total Carbohydrate: 55g
Dietary Fiber: 9g
Total Sugars: 5g
Protein: 35g
*Note: Nutrition Information is approximate and may vary based on specific ingredients used and portion sizes. Adjustments can be made for dietary preferences or restrictions.

38. Apple Crate Apple Butter

In John Steinbeck's "The Grapes of Wrath," the Joad family sustains themselves through hardship, finding solace and nourishment in simple, homemade foods. Inspired by this spirit, the "Apple Crate Apple Butter" recipe encapsulates the resourcefulness and resilience portrayed in the novel. This delicious spread captures the essence of comfort and warmth, evoking memories of home in every spoonful.

Serving: Yields approximately 3 cups of apple butter.
Preparation Time: 20 minutes
Ready Time: 8 hours (including cooking and cooling time)

Ingredients:
- 8-10 apples, preferably a mix of sweet and tart varieties (such as Granny Smith and Honeycrisp)
- 1 cup apple cider or apple juice
- 1/2 cup granulated sugar
- 1 teaspoon ground cinnamon
- 1/4 teaspoon ground cloves
- 1/4 teaspoon ground nutmeg
- Pinch of salt

Instructions:
1. Peel, core, and chop the apples into small chunks. Place them in a slow cooker or a heavy-bottomed pot.
2. Pour the apple cider or apple juice over the apples, ensuring they are mostly covered.
3. Add the sugar, ground cinnamon, ground cloves, ground nutmeg, and a pinch of salt to the pot.
4. If using a slow cooker, cook on low heat for 6-8 hours or until the apples are very soft and tender. If using a stovetop pot, simmer the mixture over low heat, stirring occasionally, for about 2-3 hours until the apples break down and become mushy.
5. Once the apples are cooked down, use an immersion blender or transfer the mixture to a blender and blend until smooth.
6. Continue cooking the apple butter uncovered, stirring occasionally, until it thickens to a spreadable consistency. This might take an additional 1-2 hours.
7. Allow the apple butter to cool completely before transferring it to clean, airtight jars or containers. Store in the refrigerator.

Nutrition Information (per 1 tablespoon serving):
- Calories: 30

- Total Fat: 0g
- Sodium: 5mg
- Total Carbohydrates: 8g
- Sugars: 7g
- Fiber: 1g
- Protein: 0g

This "Apple Crate Apple Butter" recipe celebrates the essence of resourcefulness and the comforting flavors found within the pages of "The Grapes of Wrath." Spread it on toast, swirl it into oatmeal, or use it as a flavorful topping to embrace the simple pleasures of homemade goodness.

39. Pickle Barrel Pickles

In John Steinbeck's timeless novel, "The Grapes of Wrath," the Joad family embarks on a journey filled with hardship and resilience during the Dust Bowl era. Inspired by the flavors of this era, we present the "Pickle Barrel Pickles" recipe—a zesty, crunchy delight that pays homage to the simple joys and enduring spirit of the characters in Steinbeck's masterpiece.

Serving: Makes approximately 2 quarts of pickles.
Preparation Time: 15 minutes
Ready Time: 24-48 hours (for pickles to marinate)

Ingredients:
- 3 pounds pickling cucumbers, washed and sliced into 1/4-inch rounds
- 1 large red onion, thinly sliced
- 3 cloves garlic, peeled and smashed
- 1 1/2 cups distilled white vinegar
- 1 1/2 cups water
- 1/4 cup pickling salt
- 2 tablespoons sugar
- 1 tablespoon mustard seeds
- 1 tablespoon whole black peppercorns
- 1 teaspoon dill seeds
- 1 teaspoon red pepper flakes (optional for added heat)
- 2 bay leaves

Instructions:
1. In a large mixing bowl, combine the cucumber slices, sliced red onion, and smashed garlic cloves.
2. In a saucepan, combine the white vinegar, water, pickling salt, sugar, mustard seeds, peppercorns, dill seeds, red pepper flakes (if using), and bay leaves. Bring the mixture to a boil over medium heat, stirring occasionally until the salt and sugar dissolve.
3. Once the brine is ready, carefully pour it over the cucumber mixture in the bowl. Ensure the cucumbers and onions are fully submerged in the brine. Allow the mixture to cool to room temperature.
4. Once cooled, cover the bowl with plastic wrap or a lid and refrigerate for at least 24 hours, preferably 48 hours, to allow the flavors to meld and the pickles to marinate.
5. Stir the pickles occasionally during the marination process to ensure an even distribution of flavors.
6. After the marination period, the Pickle Barrel Pickles are ready to be enjoyed. Serve them chilled as a refreshing side dish or as a crunchy addition to sandwiches.

Nutrition Information:
(Per serving, based on 1/2 cup serving size)
- Calories: 15
- Total Fat: 0g
- Cholesterol: 0mg
- Sodium: 320mg
- Total Carbohydrates: 3g
- Dietary Fiber: 1g
- Sugars: 1g
- Protein: 0g
Note: Nutrition information is approximate and may vary based on specific ingredients used. Adjustments can be made for dietary preferences or restrictions.

40. Breadline Bagels

Step into the world of the Dust Bowl with "Breadline Bagels," a humble yet hearty recipe inspired by the resilient characters in John Steinbeck's

"The Grapes of Wrath." During times of hardship, the Joad family and their fellow travelers found comfort in simple, sustenance-focused meals. These bagels are a nod to the perseverance and resourcefulness of those who endured the challenges of the Great Depression.

Serving: Makes 8 bagels
Preparation Time: 15 minutes
Ready Time: 2 hours (including rising and baking time)

Ingredients:
- 1 ½ cups warm water
- 2 tablespoons sugar
- 1 tablespoon active dry yeast
- 4 cups all-purpose flour
- 1 ½ teaspoons salt
- 1 tablespoon olive oil
- Cornmeal (for dusting)

Instructions:
1. In a bowl, combine warm water and sugar. Stir until the sugar dissolves. Sprinkle the active dry yeast over the water and let it sit for about 5 minutes until it becomes frothy.
2. In a large mixing bowl, combine the flour and salt. Make a well in the center and pour in the yeast mixture and olive oil. Mix until a dough forms.
3. Turn the dough onto a floured surface and knead for about 10 minutes until it becomes smooth and elastic.
4. Place the dough in a greased bowl, cover with a clean kitchen towel, and let it rise in a warm place for 1 hour or until it doubles in size.
5. Preheat your oven to 425°F (220°C). Bring a large pot of water to a boil and add a tablespoon of sugar.
6. Punch down the risen dough and divide it into 8 equal portions. Shape each portion into a ball and then poke a hole through the center with your thumb to form a bagel shape.
7. Boil the bagels for 1-2 minutes on each side. Remove them with a slotted spoon and place on a baking sheet dusted with cornmeal.
8. Bake for 20-25 minutes or until the bagels are golden brown.
9. Allow the bagels to cool before slicing and serving.

Nutrition Information:

(Per serving, based on 1 bagel)
- Calories: 220
- Total Fat: 1.5g
- Saturated Fat: 0.2g
- Cholesterol: 0mg
- Sodium: 440mg
- Total Carbohydrates: 44g
- Dietary Fiber: 2g
- Sugars: 3g
- Protein: 6g
Note: Nutrition information is approximate and may vary based on specific ingredients used.

41. Beanfield Barbecue

In the heart of John Steinbeck's epic novel, "The Grapes of Wrath," the Joad family finds solace in simple yet hearty meals during their arduous journey. Inspired by the resilience and resourcefulness depicted in the novel, we present the "Beanfield Barbecue" — a dish that captures the essence of sustenance and warmth. This rustic barbecue-style creation pays homage to the strength of the human spirit in the face of adversity, just as the Joads did on their way to a better life.

Serving: 4-6 servings
Preparation Time: 15 minutes
Ready Time: 1 hour 30 minutes

Ingredients:
- 2 cups dried pinto beans, soaked overnight
- 1 pound smoked sausage, sliced
- 1 onion, finely chopped
- 3 cloves garlic, minced
- 1 cup barbecue sauce
- 1/4 cup brown sugar
- 2 tablespoons mustard
- 2 tablespoons apple cider vinegar
- 1 teaspoon chili powder
- 1 teaspoon smoked paprika

- Salt and pepper to taste
- 4 cups water
- Chopped fresh parsley for garnish (optional)

Instructions:
1. Prepare the Beans:
- Drain and rinse the soaked pinto beans.
- In a large pot, combine the beans with 4 cups of water. Bring to a boil, then reduce heat and simmer for 45-60 minutes or until beans are tender. Drain and set aside.
2. Sauté the Aromatics:
- In a large skillet, sauté the sliced smoked sausage until browned. Remove the sausage and set aside.
- In the same skillet, sauté the chopped onion until translucent. Add minced garlic and cook for an additional minute.
3. Create the Sauce:
- Return the cooked sausage to the skillet with the onions and garlic.
- Add barbecue sauce, brown sugar, mustard, apple cider vinegar, chili powder, smoked paprika, salt, and pepper. Stir to combine.
4. Combine and Simmer:
- Add the cooked beans to the skillet, mixing well to coat them in the flavorful sauce.
- Simmer the mixture over low heat for 20-30 minutes, allowing the flavors to meld and the sauce to thicken.
5. Garnish and Serve:
- Garnish with chopped fresh parsley if desired.
- Serve the Beanfield Barbecue over rice, mashed potatoes, or with crusty bread.

Nutrition Information:
Note: Nutrition information is approximate and may vary based on specific ingredients and serving sizes.
- Calories per serving: 400
- Protein: 20g
- Carbohydrates: 45g
- Fiber: 10g
- Sugar: 15g
- Fat: 15g
- Saturated Fat: 5g
- Cholesterol: 30mg

- Sodium: 900mg
- Vitamin D: 2mcg
- Calcium: 100mg
- Iron: 4mg

Feel free to adjust the ingredients and measurements to suit your taste preferences. Enjoy this Beanfield Barbecue as a tribute to the enduring spirit found within the pages of "The Grapes of Wrath."

42. Jalapeño Jelly Jamboree

Embark on a culinary journey inspired by the heartland depicted in John Steinbeck's "The Grapes of Wrath" with our delightful creation, the Jalapeño Jelly Jamboree. This zesty and sweet jelly encapsulates the spirit of resourcefulness and resilience found in the novel, bringing together unexpected flavors in a true celebration of taste. Whether spread on toast, paired with cheese, or used as a glaze, this Jalapeño Jelly Jamboree is a versatile addition to your kitchen, echoing the diverse and flavorful experiences of the characters in Steinbeck's classic work.

Serving: Makes approximately 2 cups of Jalapeño Jelly.
Preparation Time: 15 minutes
Ready Time: 2 hours (including cooling time)

Ingredients:
- 1 cup finely chopped jalapeño peppers (seeds and membranes removed for milder heat)
- 2 cups green bell peppers, finely chopped
- 1 1/2 cups apple cider vinegar
- 6 cups granulated sugar
- 1 pouch (6 ounces) liquid fruit pectin
- Green food coloring (optional, for enhanced visual appeal)

Instructions:
1. Prepare Jars: Sterilize your canning jars and lids by placing them in boiling water for 10 minutes. Allow them to air dry.
2. Prepare Peppers: In a food processor, pulse the jalapeño and green bell peppers until finely chopped. Be cautious when handling the jalapeños, and consider wearing gloves.

3. Cook Peppers: In a large pot, combine the chopped peppers and apple cider vinegar. Bring the mixture to a boil over medium-high heat, stirring occasionally. Reduce the heat to low and simmer for 10 minutes.

4. Add Sugar: Gradually add the granulated sugar to the pepper mixture, stirring continuously until the sugar dissolves. Bring the mixture back to a boil and cook for an additional 10 minutes, or until it reaches a jelly-like consistency.

5. Incorporate Pectin: Stir in the liquid fruit pectin and continue boiling for 1-2 minutes. If desired, add a few drops of green food coloring to enhance the vibrant color of the jelly.

6. Check Consistency: To test if the jelly has reached the desired consistency, place a small amount on a chilled plate. Allow it to cool for a minute, then run your finger through the jelly. If it wrinkles and holds its shape, it's ready.

7. Fill Jars: Pour the hot jelly into the sterilized jars, leaving about 1/4-inch headspace. Wipe the jar rims with a clean, damp cloth to remove any residue.

8. Seal Jars: Place the sterilized lids on the jars and screw on the metal bands until fingertip-tight. Process the jars in a boiling water bath for 10 minutes to ensure proper sealing.

9. Cool and Store: Allow the jars to cool completely on a clean kitchen towel or cooling rack. Once cooled, check the seals by pressing down on the center of each lid. If it doesn't pop back, the jar is sealed. Store the sealed jars in a cool, dark place.

Nutrition Information:
(Per 1 tablespoon)
- Calories: 50
- Total Fat: 0g
- Cholesterol: 0mg
- Sodium: 0mg
- Total Carbohydrates: 13g
- Sugars: 12g
- Protein: 0g

Savor the Jalapeño Jelly Jamboree, a tribute to the enduring spirit and flavors found in the pages of "The Grapes of Wrath."

43. Prairie Pie

Inspired by John Steinbeck's classic novel, "The Grapes of Wrath," this Prairie Pie pays homage to the resilience and resourcefulness of the Joad family as they traversed the challenging landscape of the Dust Bowl. Much like the characters in the novel, this pie is a blend of humble ingredients that come together to create a comforting and flavorful dish. The simple, yet hearty, nature of this Prairie Pie reflects the spirit of survival and community found in Steinbeck's iconic work.

Serving: Serves 8
Preparation Time: 30 minutes
Ready Time: 1 hour and 30 minutes

Ingredients:
For the Crust:
- 2 1/2 cups all-purpose flour
- 1 cup unsalted butter, cold and cubed
- 1/2 cup ice water
- 1 teaspoon salt
For the Filling:
- 3 cups mixed vegetables (carrots, peas, corn, green beans), diced
- 1 onion, finely chopped
- 2 cloves garlic, minced
- 2 cups cooked chicken, shredded
- 1/4 cup all-purpose flour
- 1/4 cup unsalted butter
- 2 cups chicken broth
- 1/2 cup milk
- Salt and pepper to taste
For the Topping:
- Mashed potatoes (prepared)

Instructions:
1. Prepare the Crust:
- In a large bowl, combine the flour and salt. Add the cold, cubed butter and use a pastry cutter or your fingers to incorporate until the mixture resembles coarse crumbs.

- Gradually add the ice water, mixing until the dough comes together. Divide the dough in half, shape into discs, wrap in plastic wrap, and refrigerate for at least 30 minutes.

2. Preheat the Oven:

- Preheat your oven to 375°F (190°C).

3. Prepare the Filling:

- In a large skillet, melt the butter over medium heat. Add the chopped onion and garlic, sauté until softened.
- Add the mixed vegetables and cook until slightly tender. Stir in the shredded chicken.
- Sprinkle the flour over the mixture and stir to coat the ingredients evenly.
- Gradually pour in the chicken broth and milk, stirring constantly until the mixture thickens. Season with salt and pepper to taste. Remove from heat.

4. Assemble the Pie:

- Roll out one disc of the chilled pie crust and line a 9-inch pie dish. Pour in the prepared filling.

5. Add the Topping:

- Spread a layer of mashed potatoes over the filling, creating a rustic, textured appearance.

6. Complete the Pie:

- Roll out the second disc of pie crust and place it over the mashed potato layer. Seal the edges and make a few slits on the top to allow steam to escape.

7. Bake:

- Bake in the preheated oven for 45-50 minutes or until the crust is golden brown.

8. Serve:

- Allow the Prairie Pie to cool for 10-15 minutes before slicing and serving.

Nutrition Information:
Per Serving (1/8 of the pie):
- Calories: 450
- Total Fat: 28g
- Saturated Fat: 16g
- Cholesterol: 90mg
- Sodium: 580mg
- Total Carbohydrates: 35g

- Dietary Fiber: 3g
- Sugars: 2g
- Protein: 15g

Enjoy this hearty Prairie Pie that captures the essence of the Dust Bowl era, bringing together the flavors of hope, community, and resilience found in "The Grapes of Wrath."

44. Sourdough Starter Scones

Embark on a culinary journey inspired by John Steinbeck's "The Grapes of Wrath" with these hearty and rustic Sourdough Starter Scones. Much like the resilience of the characters in Steinbeck's classic novel, these scones showcase the enduring spirit of sourdough, bringing forth a delightful blend of flavors and textures. With a crusty exterior and a tender, tangy interior, these scones are a testament to the enduring strength found in the simplest of ingredients.

Serving: Yields 12 scones
Preparation Time: 20 minutes
Ready Time: 2 hours (includes rising time)

Ingredients:
- 1 cup active sourdough starter
- 1/2 cup whole milk
- 3 cups all-purpose flour
- 1/4 cup granulated sugar
- 1 teaspoon baking powder
- 1/2 teaspoon baking soda
- 1/2 teaspoon salt
- 1/2 cup unsalted butter, cold and cubed
- 1/2 cup dried currants or raisins (optional)
- 1 teaspoon vanilla extract

Instructions:
1. Prepare Sourdough Starter:
Ensure your sourdough starter is active and bubbly. If it's been refrigerated, take it out and let it come to room temperature.
2. Combine Wet Ingredients:

In a large mixing bowl, combine the active sourdough starter and whole milk. Stir in the vanilla extract.

3. Mix Dry Ingredients:

In a separate bowl, whisk together the all-purpose flour, granulated sugar, baking powder, baking soda, and salt.

4. Incorporate Butter:

Add the cold, cubed butter to the dry ingredients. Use your fingers or a pastry cutter to incorporate the butter until the mixture resembles coarse crumbs.

5. Combine Wet and Dry Mixtures:

Gradually add the dry ingredients to the wet ingredients, stirring until just combined. If using, fold in the dried currants or raisins.

6. Form Dough:

Turn the dough onto a floured surface and gently knead it a few times until it comes together. Pat the dough into a circle about 1 inch thick.

7. Cut Scones:

Use a floured round cutter to cut out scones from the dough. Place them on a baking sheet lined with parchment paper.

8. Rise:

Allow the scones to rise for about 1-1.5 hours, or until they have doubled in size.

9. Preheat Oven:

Preheat your oven to 400°F (200°C).

10. Bake:

Bake the scones for 15-18 minutes or until they are golden brown on top.

11. Cool:

Transfer the scones to a wire rack to cool slightly before serving.

Nutrition Information:

(Per serving - 1 scone)
- Calories: 220
- Total Fat: 8g
- Saturated Fat: 5g
- Trans Fat: 0g
- Cholesterol: 20mg
- Sodium: 240mg
- Total Carbohydrates: 33g
- Dietary Fiber: 1g
- Sugars: 5g

- Protein: 4g

These Sourdough Starter Scones embody the essence of Steinbeck's tale, offering a taste of sustenance and fortitude in every bite.

45. Vineyard Vegetable Vindaloo

Embark on a culinary journey inspired by the timeless classic, "The Grapes of Wrath" by John Steinbeck, with our delectable recipe for Vineyard Vegetable Vindaloo. This dish pays homage to the rich agricultural landscapes depicted in the novel, blending the vibrancy of seasonal vegetables with the bold flavors of vindaloo spice. Just like the novel, this recipe is a celebration of resilience and flavor, bringing together diverse elements to create a harmonious and memorable dining experience.

Serving: 4 servings
Preparation Time: 20 minutes
Ready Time: 1 hour

Ingredients:
- 2 cups eggplant, diced
- 1 cup zucchini, diced
- 1 cup bell peppers, assorted colors, diced
- 1 cup cherry tomatoes, halved
- 1 cup red onion, diced
- 3 cloves garlic, minced
- 1 tablespoon ginger, minced
- 2 tablespoons vegetable oil
- 1 cup tomato puree
- 1/4 cup red wine vinegar
- 2 tablespoons vindaloo spice blend
- 1 teaspoon turmeric
- 1 teaspoon cumin powder
- 1 teaspoon coriander powder
- 1/2 teaspoon cayenne pepper (adjust to taste)
- Salt to taste
- Fresh cilantro for garnish

Instructions:
1. In a large pan, heat vegetable oil over medium heat. Add minced garlic and ginger, sauté until fragrant.
2. Add diced red onion and cook until translucent. Add the eggplant, zucchini, and bell peppers. Sauté for 5-7 minutes until vegetables are slightly tender.
3. Stir in the cherry tomatoes, tomato puree, red wine vinegar, vindaloo spice blend, turmeric, cumin powder, coriander powder, cayenne pepper, and salt. Mix well to coat the vegetables evenly with the spices.
4. Reduce heat to low, cover, and let the vegetables simmer for 30-40 minutes, allowing the flavors to meld and the vegetables to become tender.
5. Taste and adjust the seasoning if necessary. If you prefer a spicier dish, add more cayenne pepper.
6. Garnish with fresh cilantro before serving.

Nutrition Information (per serving):
- Calories: 220
- Protein: 4g
- Fat: 12g
- Carbohydrates: 25g
- Fiber: 7g
- Sugar: 11g
- Sodium: 480mg

Immerse yourself in the flavors of the vineyard with this hearty and aromatic Vineyard Vegetable Vindaloo. Perfect for sharing with loved ones, this dish brings a taste of both the bountiful harvest and the enduring spirit found within the pages of "The Grapes of Wrath."

46. Dust Bowl Dal

In the heart of John Steinbeck's iconic novel, "The Grapes of Wrath," the Dust Bowl era is vividly portrayed, revealing the harsh realities faced by migrant families. Inspired by the resilience and simplicity of the characters in the novel, we present the "Dust Bowl Dal" — a nourishing and wholesome dish that pays homage to the endurance and strength of those who weathered the storm. This dal is a humble yet flavorful blend of lentils and spices, reflecting the resourcefulness of individuals during challenging times.

Serving: 4 servings
Preparation Time: 15 minutes
Ready Time: 45 minutes

Ingredients:
- 1 cup red lentils, washed and drained
- 4 cups water
- 2 tablespoons vegetable oil
- 1 large onion, finely chopped
- 3 cloves garlic, minced
- 1 tablespoon ginger, grated
- 1 teaspoon cumin seeds
- 1 teaspoon ground turmeric
- 1 teaspoon coriander powder
- 1 teaspoon garam masala
- 1/2 teaspoon chili powder (adjust to taste)
- 1 can (14 oz) diced tomatoes
- Salt to taste
- Fresh cilantro, chopped (for garnish)
- Lemon wedges (for serving)

Instructions:
1. In a large pot, combine the washed red lentils and water. Bring to a boil, then reduce heat to simmer and cook until lentils are tender, about 20-25 minutes.
2. In a separate pan, heat vegetable oil over medium heat. Add cumin seeds and let them sizzle for a few seconds.
3. Add chopped onions to the pan and sauté until golden brown.
4. Stir in minced garlic and grated ginger, cooking for an additional 2 minutes until fragrant.
5. Add ground turmeric, coriander powder, garam masala, and chili powder to the onion mixture. Cook for another 2 minutes, allowing the spices to bloom.
6. Pour in the can of diced tomatoes (with juices) and cook until the oil starts to separate from the tomato-spice mixture.

7. Combine the spiced tomato mixture with the cooked lentils. Season with salt to taste and let the dal simmer for an additional 15-20 minutes, allowing the flavors to meld.

8. Garnish with fresh cilantro and serve hot with rice or your favorite bread. Add a squeeze of lemon for a burst of freshness.

Nutrition Information:
(Per Serving)
- Calories: 250
- Protein: 15g
- Fat: 7g
- Carbohydrates: 35g
- Fiber: 10g
- Sugar: 4g
- Sodium: 600mg

Embrace the simplicity and heartiness of the Dust Bowl Dal, a dish that brings warmth and nourishment to your table, echoing the enduring spirit of those who faced adversity during the Dust Bowl era.

47. Grilled Grapefruit

Step into the world of "The Grapes of Wrath" with a refreshing and tangy twist on a classic fruit. Grilled Grapefruit captures the essence of resilience and simplicity found in the novel, offering a burst of flavor that resonates with the struggles and triumphs of the Joad family. This dish is a celebration of the bittersweet journey, just like the novel itself.

Serving: 2 servings
Preparation Time: 10 minutes
Ready Time: 15 minutes

Ingredients:
- 2 large grapefruits
- 2 tablespoons honey
- 1 teaspoon ground cinnamon
- 1 tablespoon melted butter
- A pinch of salt
- Fresh mint leaves for garnish (optional)

Instructions:
1. Preheat the Grill:
- Preheat your grill to medium-high heat.
2. Prepare the Grapefruit:
- Cut each grapefruit in half.
- Using a knife, carefully cut around each segment of the grapefruit to loosen it from the membrane.
3. Brush with Honey and Butter:
- In a small bowl, mix the melted butter, honey, ground cinnamon, and a pinch of salt.
- Brush the honey-cinnamon mixture generously over the exposed surface of each grapefruit half.
4. Grill the Grapefruit:
- Place the grapefruit halves on the preheated grill, cut side down.
- Grill for about 3-5 minutes, or until you see grill marks and the fruit starts to caramelize.
5. Serve:
- Remove the grilled grapefruit halves from the grill and place them on a serving platter.
- Optionally, garnish with fresh mint leaves.
6. Enjoy:
- Serve the Grilled Grapefruit immediately while it's still warm. The heat from the grill enhances the natural sweetness of the fruit, and the honey-cinnamon glaze adds a delightful depth of flavor.

Nutrition Information:
(Per Serving)
- Calories: 120
- Total Fat: 3g
- Saturated Fat: 2g
- Trans Fat: 0g
- Cholesterol: 10mg
- Sodium: 60mg
- Total Carbohydrates: 26g
- Dietary Fiber: 4g
- Sugars: 20g
- Protein: 1g

This Grilled Grapefruit recipe is a tribute to the enduring spirit found in "The Grapes of Wrath" — simple, hearty, and full of flavor. Enjoy this dish as a reminder of the strength and resilience that can be found even in the face of adversity.

48. Pickle Barrel Pancakes

In John Steinbeck's iconic novel "The Grapes of Wrath," food represents sustenance and resilience in the face of adversity. Inspired by this theme, Pickle Barrel Pancakes symbolize resourcefulness, utilizing simple ingredients to create a hearty and comforting meal reminiscent of the novel's spirit.

Serving: Makes approximately 8 pancakes
Preparation time: 10 minutes
Ready time: 20 minutes

Ingredients:
- 1 cup all-purpose flour
- 1 tablespoon granulated sugar
- 1 teaspoon baking powder
- 1/2 teaspoon baking soda
- 1/2 teaspoon salt
- 1 cup buttermilk
- 1 large egg
- 2 tablespoons unsalted butter, melted
- 1/2 cup chopped dill pickles
- 1/4 cup grated cheddar cheese
- Cooking oil or butter for greasing the pan

Instructions:
1. In a mixing bowl, whisk together the flour, sugar, baking powder, baking soda, and salt.
2. In another bowl, whisk the buttermilk and egg until well combined.
3. Gradually pour the wet ingredients into the dry ingredients, stirring until just combined. Avoid overmixing; a few lumps are okay.
4. Gently fold in the melted butter, chopped dill pickles, and grated cheddar cheese into the batter.
5. Heat a non-stick skillet or griddle over medium heat. Add a small amount of oil or butter to grease the surface.

6. Pour 1/4 cup of batter onto the skillet for each pancake. Cook until bubbles form on the surface, then flip and cook until golden brown on both sides, about 2-3 minutes per side.

7. Remove the pancakes from the skillet and keep warm. Repeat with the remaining batter.

8. Serve the Pickle Barrel Pancakes warm, topped with additional chopped pickles or a dollop of sour cream, if desired.

Nutrition Information: *(per serving)*

Note: Nutritional values are approximate and may vary based on specific ingredients used.

- Calories: 170 kcal
- Fat: 7g
- Saturated Fat: 4g
- Cholesterol: 45mg
- Sodium: 480mg
- Carbohydrates: 21g
- Fiber: 1g
- Sugar: 3g
- Protein: 5g

These Pickle Barrel Pancakes capture the essence of resilience and resourcefulness found in "The Grapes of Wrath." Enjoy their savory, tangy flavor as a nod to the strength and endurance of the characters in Steinbeck's masterpiece.

49. Barley Biscuits

In John Steinbeck's "The Grapes of Wrath," the resilience and resourcefulness of families during challenging times are celebrated. Barley biscuits, a humble yet hearty staple, embody the spirit of making the most of what's available. These rustic biscuits offer a comforting taste of sustenance and perseverance, echoing the resilience found within the pages of this classic novel.

Serving: Makes about 12 biscuits
Preparation Time: 15 minutes
Ready Time: 35 minutes

Ingredients:
- 1 cup barley flour
- 1 cup all-purpose flour
- 1 tablespoon baking powder
- 1/2 teaspoon salt
- 1/4 cup cold unsalted butter, cut into small pieces
- 1/2 cup cold buttermilk
- 1 tablespoon honey or molasses (optional, for a touch of sweetness)

Instructions:
1. Preheat Oven: Preheat your oven to 400°F (200°C). Line a baking sheet with parchment paper or lightly grease it.
2. Mix Dry Ingredients: In a large mixing bowl, combine the barley flour, all-purpose flour, baking powder, and salt. Stir until well mixed.
3. Incorporate Butter: Add the cold butter pieces to the dry ingredients. Use a pastry cutter or your fingertips to work the butter into the flour mixture until it resembles coarse crumbs.
4. Add Wet Ingredients: Pour in the cold buttermilk and honey or molasses (if using). Stir gently until the dough just comes together. Be careful not to overmix; the dough should be slightly sticky.
5. Shape Biscuits: Transfer the dough onto a lightly floured surface. Pat it down to about 1-inch thickness. Use a biscuit cutter or a floured glass to cut out rounds of dough. Place the biscuits on the prepared baking sheet.
6. Bake: Bake the biscuits in the preheated oven for 12-15 minutes or until they turn golden brown on top.
7. Serve: Once baked, let the barley biscuits cool slightly on a wire rack. Serve warm with a spread of butter, jam, or alongside soups and stews for a nourishing meal.

Nutrition Information (per biscuit):
- Calories: 120
- Total Fat: 4g
- Saturated Fat: 2.5g
- Cholesterol: 10mg
- Sodium: 220mg
- Total Carbohydrates: 18g
- Dietary Fiber: 2g
- Sugars: 1g
- Protein: 3g

These barley biscuits, reminiscent of simpler times, embody the essence of endurance and sustenance found in the pages of "The Grapes of Wrath." Enjoy these wholesome biscuits as a tribute to the indomitable spirit of survival and hope that resonates throughout Steinbeck's masterpiece.

50. Tomato Tin Tuna

"Tomato Tin Tuna" pays homage to the resourcefulness depicted in Steinbeck's "The Grapes of Wrath." This simple yet flavorful dish captures the essence of making do with what's available, much like the Joad family did during their journey. Using pantry staples, it delivers a delicious blend of flavors that comfort and sustain.

Serving: 4 servings
Preparation time: 10 minutes
Ready time: 15 minutes

Ingredients:
- 2 cans (5 oz each) of tuna in olive oil
- 1 can (14 oz) diced tomatoes
- 1 small onion, finely chopped
- 2 cloves garlic, minced
- 1 teaspoon dried oregano
- 1 teaspoon dried basil
- Salt and pepper to taste
- 2 tablespoons olive oil
- Cooked pasta or crusty bread (optional, for serving)

Instructions:
1. Heat olive oil in a skillet over medium heat. Add the chopped onion and minced garlic. Sauté until the onion turns translucent, about 3-4 minutes.
2. Add the canned diced tomatoes (with their juices) to the skillet. Stir in the dried oregano, dried basil, salt, and pepper. Let it simmer for 5 minutes, allowing the flavors to meld.

3. Gently add the canned tuna with its oil to the skillet. Break up the tuna with a fork and stir to combine with the tomato mixture. Simmer for an additional 5 minutes, ensuring everything is heated through.
4. Taste and adjust seasoning if needed. Remove from heat.

Nutrition Information (per serving):
- Calories: 220
- Total Fat: 12g
- Saturated Fat: 2g
- Cholesterol: 35mg
- Sodium: 450mg
- Total Carbohydrate: 7g
- Dietary Fiber: 2g
- Sugars: 4g
- Protein: 21g

Serve the Tomato Tin Tuna over cooked pasta or alongside crusty bread for a satisfying meal that embodies the resourcefulness and resilience reflected in "The Grapes of Wrath."

51. Grapes of Wrath Granola

In the spirit of John Steinbeck's iconic novel, "The Grapes of Wrath," we present the "Grapes of Wrath Granola." This hearty and wholesome granola is inspired by the resilience and fortitude of the Joad family as they journeyed through the Dust Bowl era. Packed with nutritious ingredients, this granola captures the essence of survival and hope, making it a perfect addition to your breakfast or snack repertoire.

Serving: Makes approximately 8 servings
Preparation Time: 15 minutes
Ready Time: 45 minutes

Ingredients:
- 3 cups old-fashioned rolled oats
- 1 cup almonds, chopped
- 1 cup walnuts, chopped
- 1/2 cup sunflower seeds
- 1/2 cup pumpkin seeds

- 1/2 cup unsweetened shredded coconut
- 1/2 cup raisins
- 1/2 cup dried cranberries
- 1/4 cup coconut oil, melted
- 1/4 cup maple syrup
- 1 teaspoon vanilla extract
- 1/2 teaspoon ground cinnamon
- 1/4 teaspoon salt

Instructions:
1. Preheat your oven to 325°F (163°C) and line a baking sheet with parchment paper.
2. In a large mixing bowl, combine the rolled oats, chopped almonds, chopped walnuts, sunflower seeds, pumpkin seeds, shredded coconut, raisins, and dried cranberries. Mix well to distribute the ingredients evenly.
3. In a small bowl, whisk together the melted coconut oil, maple syrup, vanilla extract, ground cinnamon, and salt until well combined.
4. Pour the wet mixture over the dry ingredients and stir until everything is evenly coated.
5. Spread the granola mixture evenly onto the prepared baking sheet, pressing it down slightly with a spatula.
6. Bake in the preheated oven for 30-35 minutes or until the granola is golden brown, stirring halfway through to ensure even cooking.
7. Remove from the oven and allow the granola to cool completely on the baking sheet. It will continue to crisp up as it cools.
8. Once cooled, break the granola into clusters and transfer to an airtight container for storage.

Nutrition Information:
(Per Serving)
- Calories: 320
- Total Fat: 21g
- Saturated Fat: 7g
- Cholesterol: 0mg
- Sodium: 60mg
- Total Carbohydrates: 28g
- Dietary Fiber: 5g
- Sugars: 10g
- Protein: 8g

Enjoy your "Grapes of Wrath Granola" as a symbol of resilience and nourishment in the face of adversity!

52. Cornfield Cobbler

In the heart of John Steinbeck's "The Grapes of Wrath," the struggles and triumphs of the Joad family reflect the resilience of the human spirit in the face of adversity. Inspired by the agrarian setting and the enduring spirit of the characters, we present the "Cornfield Cobbler," a dish that pays homage to the fertile fields of the Dust Bowl. This comforting dessert embodies the essence of hope and sustenance found amidst hardship.

Serving: 6-8 servings
Preparation Time: 20 minutes
Ready Time: 45 minutes

Ingredients:
- 4 cups fresh or frozen corn kernels
- 1 cup all-purpose flour
- 1 cup granulated sugar
- 1 tablespoon baking powder
- 1/2 teaspoon salt
- 1 cup whole milk
- 1/2 cup unsalted butter, melted
- 1 teaspoon vanilla extract
- 1/2 teaspoon ground cinnamon
- 1/4 teaspoon ground nutmeg
- 1/4 cup brown sugar (for topping)
- Vanilla ice cream (optional, for serving)

Instructions:
1. Preheat your oven to 375°F (190°C). Grease a baking dish with butter or cooking spray.
2. In a large mixing bowl, combine the corn kernels, flour, granulated sugar, baking powder, and salt.
3. In a separate bowl, whisk together the milk, melted butter, vanilla extract, cinnamon, and nutmeg.

4. Pour the wet ingredients into the bowl with the dry ingredients. Stir until just combined. The batter will be lumpy, and that's okay.
5. Pour the batter into the prepared baking dish, spreading it evenly.
6. Sprinkle the brown sugar over the top of the batter.
7. Bake in the preheated oven for 40-45 minutes or until the top is golden brown, and a toothpick inserted into the center comes out clean.
8. Allow the Cornfield Cobbler to cool for a few minutes before serving. Optionally, serve warm with a scoop of vanilla ice cream.

Nutrition Information:
(Per serving, based on 8 servings)
- Calories: 380
- Total Fat: 15g
- Saturated Fat: 9g
- Trans Fat: 0g
- Cholesterol: 40mg
- Sodium: 370mg
- Total Carbohydrates: 59g
- Dietary Fiber: 3g
- Sugars: 35g
- Protein: 4g
The Cornfield Cobbler captures the essence of sustenance and resilience, making it a fitting tribute to the enduring spirit found within the pages of "The Grapes of Wrath."

53. Oakie Olive Oil Omelette

In the spirit of John Steinbeck's iconic novel, "The Grapes of Wrath," we present the Oakie Olive Oil Omelette—an homage to the resilience and resourcefulness of the Okies during the Dust Bowl era. This hearty and simple omelette captures the essence of survival and sustenance, showcasing the humble ingredients available to those who sought a better life on their journey westward.

Serving: Serves 2
Preparation Time: 10 minutes
Ready Time: 15 minutes

Ingredients:

- 4 large eggs
- 2 tablespoons Oakie Olive Oil
- 1/4 cup diced onions
- 1/4 cup diced bell peppers (any color)
- 1/4 cup diced tomatoes
- 1/4 cup shredded cheddar cheese
- Salt and pepper to taste
- Fresh herbs for garnish (optional)

Instructions:

1. Prepare the Ingredients:
- Dice the onions, bell peppers, and tomatoes.
- Shred the cheddar cheese.
- Crack the eggs into a bowl and beat them until well combined.
2. Sauté Vegetables:
- Heat Oakie Olive Oil in a non-stick skillet over medium heat.
- Sauté the diced onions and bell peppers until they are softened and slightly caramelized.
3. Add Tomatoes:
- Add the diced tomatoes to the skillet and cook for an additional 1-2 minutes, allowing them to soften.
4. Beat and Pour Eggs:
- Pour the beaten eggs into the skillet over the sautéed vegetables.
5. Season and Cook:
- Season with salt and pepper to taste.
- Allow the eggs to set slightly around the edges, and then gently stir, lifting the edges to let the uncooked egg flow underneath.
6. Add Cheese:
- Sprinkle the shredded cheddar cheese over one half of the omelette.
7. Fold and Serve:
- Once the eggs are fully set but still moist, fold the omelette in half with a spatula.
- Slide the Oakie Olive Oil Omelette onto a plate.
8. Garnish and Enjoy:
- Garnish with fresh herbs if desired.
- Serve hot and savor the flavors inspired by the resilience of the Okies in "The Grapes of Wrath."

Nutrition Information (per serving):

- Calories: 280
- Protein: 16g
- Fat: 22g
- Carbohydrates: 4g
- Fiber: 1g
- Sugar: 2g
- Sodium: 320mg

Note: Nutrition information is approximate and may vary based on specific ingredients used.

54. Bank Note Borscht

In John Steinbeck's epic tale "The Grapes of Wrath," food often symbolizes resilience and resourcefulness in the face of adversity. Inspired by the indomitable spirit of survival, "Bank Note Borscht" represents a humble yet flavorful dish that embodies sustenance during trying times. This hearty soup reflects the resourceful use of available ingredients, mirroring the Joad family's endurance through hardship and their ability to create nourishing meals from limited resources.

Serving: 6 servings
Preparation Time: 20 minutes
Ready Time: 1 hour 30 minutes

Ingredients:
- 2 tablespoons olive oil
- 1 onion, finely chopped
- 2 cloves garlic, minced
- 2 medium beets, peeled and grated
- 2 carrots, peeled and diced
- 2 potatoes, peeled and cubed
- 4 cups vegetable or beef broth
- 1 can (14 oz) diced tomatoes
- 1 tablespoon tomato paste
- 1 bay leaf
- 1 teaspoon paprika
- 1 teaspoon caraway seeds (optional)
- Salt and pepper to taste

- 1 tablespoon red wine vinegar
- Sour cream or yogurt, for serving
- Chopped fresh dill, for garnish

Instructions:
1. Heat olive oil in a large pot over medium heat. Add the chopped onion and garlic, sauté until fragrant and translucent, about 3-4 minutes.
2. Stir in the grated beets, diced carrots, and cubed potatoes. Cook for another 5 minutes, stirring occasionally.
3. Pour in the vegetable or beef broth, diced tomatoes, tomato paste, bay leaf, paprika, caraway seeds (if using), salt, and pepper. Bring the mixture to a boil.
4. Once boiling, reduce the heat to low, cover the pot, and let the soup simmer for about 1 hour until the vegetables are tender, stirring occasionally.
5. Remove the bay leaf from the soup. Stir in the red wine vinegar, adjusting the seasoning if needed.
6. Ladle the borscht into serving bowls. Top each bowl with a dollop of sour cream or yogurt and a sprinkle of fresh dill for garnish.

Nutrition Information (per serving):
- Calories: 150
- Total Fat: 5g
- Sodium: 800mg
- Total Carbohydrates: 23g
- Dietary Fiber: 5g
- Sugars: 8g
- Protein: 4g

This Bank Note Borscht is a tribute to the resilience found in the pages of "The Grapes of Wrath," embodying the spirit of endurance and resourcefulness in challenging times.

55. Peach Pit Popcorn

In John Steinbeck's "The Grapes of Wrath," the Peach Pit Popcorn symbolizes resilience and resourcefulness amidst hardship. This recipe celebrates the ingenuity of making a delightful snack out of something seemingly unassuming. With its sweet and savory flavors, Peach Pit

Popcorn mirrors the novel's themes of making the most out of what's available, turning humble ingredients into something extraordinary.

Serving: Serves 4
Preparation Time: 10 minutes
Ready Time: 20 minutes

Ingredients:
- 2 tablespoons vegetable oil
- 1/2 cup popcorn kernels
- 1/4 cup peach pit powder (dried and finely ground peach pits)
- 2 tablespoons unsalted butter, melted
- 2 tablespoons powdered sugar
- 1/2 teaspoon salt

Instructions:
1. Prepare the Peach Pit Powder: Rinse and dry peach pits thoroughly. Once dry, carefully crack the pits open and remove the kernels inside. Place the kernels in a dehydrator or in an oven set to its lowest temperature until completely dried out. Grind the dried kernels into a fine powder using a blender or food processor. Set aside.
2. Heat the oil in a large pot over medium heat. Add the popcorn kernels and cover with a lid, leaving a small gap for steam to escape.
3. Gently shake the pot occasionally to ensure even popping. Once the popping slows down, remove from heat and let it sit for a minute to ensure all kernels have popped.
4. Transfer the popcorn to a large mixing bowl.
5. In a separate small bowl, combine the peach pit powder, powdered sugar, and salt.
6. Drizzle the melted butter over the popcorn, tossing gently to coat evenly.
7. Sprinkle the peach pit powder mixture over the buttered popcorn and toss again until well coated.
8. Allow the popcorn to cool slightly before serving.

Nutrition Information (per serving):
- Calories: 180
- Total Fat: 10g
- Saturated Fat: 4g
- Cholesterol: 15mg

- Sodium: 300mg
- Total Carbohydrate: 20g
- Dietary Fiber: 4g
- Sugars: 3g
- Protein: 3g

Enjoy the Peach Pit Popcorn as a testament to resourcefulness and the ability to find joy even in the simplest of things, just as the characters in "The Grapes of Wrath" did amidst adversity.

56. Cotton Candy Cabbage Rolls

In "The Grapes of Wrath," Steinbeck vividly portrays the resilience and resourcefulness of families during challenging times. Inspired by this spirit, the Cotton Candy Cabbage Rolls symbolize the fusion of humble ingredients into a delightful dish. These rolls blend the nostalgia of traditional cabbage rolls with a whimsical twist, reminiscent of the hope found amidst adversity.

Serving: 6 servings
Preparation time: 30 minutes
Ready time: 1 hour 30 minutes

Ingredients:
- 1 large head of cabbage
- 1 cup uncooked white rice
- 1 pound ground beef
- 1 onion, finely chopped
- 2 cloves garlic, minced
- 1 can (14 ounces) crushed tomatoes
- 1 tablespoon tomato paste
- 1 teaspoon paprika
- Salt and pepper to taste
- 1 cup chicken or vegetable broth
- 1/2 cup sour cream (optional, for serving)
- Fresh parsley for garnish

Instructions:

1. Prepare the Cabbage: Bring a large pot of water to a boil. Core the cabbage and carefully place it in the boiling water, letting it cook for about 5-7 minutes until the outer leaves are softened. Remove the cabbage from the water and carefully peel off the softened leaves. Set aside.

2. Cook the Rice: In a separate saucepan, cook the white rice according to package instructions. Set aside once done.

3. Prepare the Filling: In a skillet over medium heat, cook the ground beef until browned. Add in the chopped onions and garlic, sautéing until they become translucent. Stir in the cooked rice, crushed tomatoes, tomato paste, paprika, salt, and pepper. Cook for an additional 5-7 minutes until well combined. Set aside.

4. Assemble the Rolls: Preheat the oven to 350°F (175°C). Take each cabbage leaf and place a spoonful of the beef and rice mixture at the base of the leaf. Roll it up, tucking in the sides as you go, similar to rolling a burrito. Repeat with the remaining cabbage leaves and filling.

5. Bake the Rolls: Place the cabbage rolls seam-side down in a baking dish. Pour the chicken or vegetable broth over the rolls. Cover the dish with foil and bake in the preheated oven for 45-50 minutes until the cabbage is tender and the filling is cooked through.

6. Serve: Once done, remove from the oven. Optionally, serve the cotton candy cabbage rolls with a dollop of sour cream on top and a sprinkle of fresh parsley for garnish.

Nutrition Information (per serving, without optional toppings):
- Calories: 320
- Total Fat: 12g
- Saturated Fat: 5g
- Cholesterol: 45mg
- Sodium: 480mg
- Total Carbohydrate: 35g
- Dietary Fiber: 4g
- Sugars: 6g
- Protein: 18g

This dish beautifully combines the simplicity of staple ingredients with a touch of creativity, embodying the perseverance and innovation found in the face of adversity, much like the characters in "The Grapes of Wrath."

57. Oakie Oxtail Stew

Step into the pages of John Steinbeck's "The Grapes of Wrath" with the hearty and soul-warming Oakie Oxtail Stew. Inspired by the resilience and strength of the Joad family, this comforting dish captures the essence of the struggle and triumph of the human spirit. Let the robust flavors and rich textures transport you to the dusty landscapes of the Dust Bowl era as you savor every spoonful of this wholesome stew.

Serving: 4-6 servings
Preparation Time: 30 minutes
Ready Time: 4 hours

Ingredients:
- 2 lbs oxtail, cut into segments
- 2 tablespoons vegetable oil
- 1 large onion, finely chopped
- 3 cloves garlic, minced
- 2 carrots, peeled and diced
- 2 celery stalks, diced
- 1 cup red wine (Cabernet Sauvignon or Merlot)
- 2 cups beef broth
- 1 can (14 oz) diced tomatoes
- 2 bay leaves
- 1 teaspoon dried thyme
- Salt and pepper to taste
- 1 cup potatoes, peeled and diced
- 1 cup butternut squash, peeled and diced
- Chopped fresh parsley for garnish

Instructions:
1. Brown the Oxtail:
- In a large pot or Dutch oven, heat vegetable oil over medium-high heat. Brown the oxtail segments on all sides until they develop a rich, caramelized color. Remove them from the pot and set aside.
2. Sauté Aromatics:
- In the same pot, add chopped onions and garlic. Sauté until softened and aromatic. Add diced carrots and celery, cooking for an additional 3-5 minutes until the vegetables begin to soften.
3. Deglaze with Red Wine:

- Pour in the red wine, scraping the bottom of the pot to release any flavorful bits. Allow the wine to simmer and reduce by half.

4. Combine Ingredients:
- Return the browned oxtail to the pot. Add beef broth, diced tomatoes, bay leaves, dried thyme, salt, and pepper. Bring the mixture to a gentle boil.

5. Simmer:
- Reduce the heat to low, cover the pot, and let the stew simmer for approximately 2 hours, or until the oxtail begins to tenderize.

6. Add Vegetables:
- Stir in diced potatoes and butternut squash. Continue simmering for an additional 1-2 hours until the vegetables and oxtail are fork-tender, and the flavors meld together.

7. Adjust Seasoning:
- Taste the stew and adjust salt and pepper as needed. Remove bay leaves.

8. Serve:
- Ladle the Oakie Oxtail Stew into bowls, garnish with chopped fresh parsley, and serve hot. Pair with crusty bread or a simple green salad for a complete meal.

Nutrition Information:
(Per serving, based on 6 servings)
- Calories: 450
- Protein: 30g
- Fat: 25g
- Carbohydrates: 20g
- Fiber: 4g

Indulge in the Oakie Oxtail Stew, a dish that pays homage to the enduring spirit depicted in "The Grapes of Wrath," and savor the flavors of a bygone era.

58. Migrant Mustard Greens

As we journey through the pages of "The Grapes of Wrath" by John Steinbeck, we encounter a poignant narrative of struggle, resilience, and the search for a better life. Inspired by the indomitable spirit of the migrant families depicted in the novel, our "Migrant Mustard Greens" recipe pays homage to the simple yet robust flavors that sustained these characters on their arduous journey. Packed with nutrient-rich ingredients, this dish serves as a symbol of fortitude and the enduring human spirit.

Serving: 4 servings
Preparation Time: 15 minutes
Ready Time: 30 minutes

Ingredients:
- 1 pound fresh mustard greens, washed and chopped
- 2 tablespoons olive oil
- 1 medium onion, finely chopped
- 2 cloves garlic, minced
- 1 teaspoon red pepper flakes (adjust to taste)
- Salt and black pepper to taste
- 1 cup cherry tomatoes, halved
- 1 can (15 ounces) cannellini beans, drained and rinsed
- 1 lemon, juiced
- Grated Parmesan cheese for garnish (optional)

Instructions:
1. Prepare Mustard Greens: Wash the mustard greens thoroughly and chop them into bite-sized pieces, discarding tough stems.
2. Sauté Aromatics: In a large skillet, heat olive oil over medium heat. Add chopped onions and garlic, sautéing until fragrant and translucent.
3. Spice it Up: Sprinkle red pepper flakes into the skillet, adjusting the quantity to your spice preference. Season with salt and black pepper to taste.
4. Add Greens: Incorporate the chopped mustard greens into the skillet. Toss them gently until wilted but still vibrant green.
5. Introduce Tomatoes and Beans: Add halved cherry tomatoes and drained cannellini beans to the skillet. Stir well to combine all the ingredients.
6. Lemon Zest: Squeeze the juice of one lemon over the greens mixture. The citrusy zing will brighten up the dish.
7. Simmer: Allow the mixture to simmer for 10-15 minutes, letting the flavors meld together.

8. Serve: Once the mustard greens are tender and the flavors have melded, serve the dish hot. Optionally, garnish with grated Parmesan cheese for an extra layer of richness.

Nutrition Information:
(Per serving)
- Calories: 180
- Protein: 8g
- Carbohydrates: 22g
- Fiber: 7g
- Fat: 8g
- Saturated Fat: 1g
- Cholesterol: 0mg
- Sodium: 320mg

This "Migrant Mustard Greens" dish captures the essence of resilience in a bowl, providing both sustenance and a connection to the characters that traversed the challenging landscape of "The Grapes of Wrath."

59. Boxcar Buttermilk Biscuits

Step into the world of "The Grapes of Wrath" by John Steinbeck with a recipe inspired by the humble and hearty meals shared by the Joad family on their journey to California. These Boxcar Buttermilk Biscuits pay homage to the resourcefulness and resilience of those who sought a better life during the Dust Bowl era. Simple yet satisfying, these biscuits are a testament to the enduring spirit of the human soul.

Serving: Makes 12 biscuits
Preparation Time: 15 minutes
Ready Time: 25 minutes

Ingredients:
- 2 cups all-purpose flour
- 1 tablespoon baking powder
- 1/2 teaspoon baking soda
- 1/2 teaspoon salt
- 1/2 cup unsalted butter, cold and cubed
- 1 cup buttermilk, cold

- 1 tablespoon honey (optional, for a touch of sweetness)

Instructions:
1. Preheat your oven to 450°F (230°C). Line a baking sheet with parchment paper.
2. In a large mixing bowl, whisk together the flour, baking powder, baking soda, and salt.
3. Add the cold, cubed butter to the dry ingredients. Using a pastry cutter or your fingertips, work the butter into the flour mixture until it resembles coarse crumbs.
4. Make a well in the center of the mixture and pour in the cold buttermilk. Gently stir until just combined. If desired, add honey for a subtle sweetness.
5. Turn the dough out onto a floured surface and knead it lightly a few times until it comes together. Pat the dough into a rectangle about 1 inch thick.
6. Using a floured biscuit cutter, cut out biscuits and place them on the prepared baking sheet, ensuring they are close but not touching.
7. Bake in the preheated oven for 12-15 minutes or until the biscuits are golden brown on top.
8. Remove from the oven and let them cool slightly on a wire rack. Serve warm with butter, jam, or as a side to your favorite hearty dish.

Nutrition Information:
(Per serving - 1 biscuit)
- Calories: 150
- Total Fat: 8g
- Saturated Fat: 5g
- Cholesterol: 20mg
- Sodium: 300mg
- Total Carbohydrates: 18g
- Dietary Fiber: 1g
- Sugars: 2g
- Protein: 3g

Enjoy these Boxcar Buttermilk Biscuits as a tribute to the strength and perseverance found in the pages of "The Grapes of Wrath."

60. Weedpatch Waldorf Salad

Step back in time to the Dust Bowl era with the Weedpatch Waldorf Salad, a delightful dish inspired by John Steinbeck's "The Grapes of Wrath." Named after the Weedpatch Camp, a government-sponsored migrant camp mentioned in the novel, this salad pays homage to the resilience and resourcefulness of those who faced adversity during the Great Depression. Crisp and refreshing, this salad is a nod to the simplicity and creativity that can arise from humble circumstances.

Serving: 4 servings
Preparation Time: 15 minutes
Ready Time: 15 minutes

Ingredients:
- 2 cups crisp green apples, diced
- 1 cup celery, thinly sliced
- 1 cup red seedless grapes, halved
- 1/2 cup walnuts, toasted and chopped
- 1/2 cup mayonnaise
- 2 tablespoons sour cream
- 1 tablespoon honey
- 1 teaspoon lemon juice
- Salt and pepper to taste
- Fresh parsley for garnish (optional)

Instructions:
1. Prepare the Ingredients:
- Dice the green apples.
- Thinly slice the celery.
- Halve the red grapes.
- Toast and chop the walnuts.
2. Make the Dressing:
- In a small bowl, whisk together mayonnaise, sour cream, honey, lemon juice, salt, and pepper. Adjust the seasoning to taste.
3. Combine the Ingredients:
- In a large mixing bowl, combine the diced apples, sliced celery, halved grapes, and chopped walnuts.
4. Add the Dressing:

- Pour the dressing over the salad ingredients and gently toss until everything is well coated.
5. Chill and Serve:
- Refrigerate the Weedpatch Waldorf Salad for at least 1 hour to allow the flavors to meld.
6. Garnish and Serve:
- Before serving, garnish with fresh parsley if desired. Serve chilled.

Nutrition Information:
(Per Serving)
- Calories: 280
- Total Fat: 20g
- Saturated Fat: 3g
- Trans Fat: 0g
- Cholesterol: 10mg
- Sodium: 120mg
- Total Carbohydrates: 25g
- Dietary Fiber: 4g
- Sugars: 18g
- Protein: 2g

Enjoy the Weedpatch Waldorf Salad as a tribute to the enduring spirit of those who found solace and strength in the face of challenges during the Dust Bowl era.

61. Farmstead Flatbread

In the heart of John Steinbeck's epic novel, "The Grapes of Wrath," the Joad family traverses the Dust Bowl in search of a better life. Inspired by the resilience and simplicity of farmstead living, we present the "Farmstead Flatbread." This rustic recipe pays homage to the hardworking spirit of those who toiled the land during the Great Depression, using straightforward ingredients to create a wholesome and hearty dish.

Serving: 4-6 people
Preparation Time: 15 minutes
Ready Time: 30 minutes

Ingredients:
- 2 cups all-purpose flour
- 1 teaspoon baking powder
- 1/2 teaspoon salt
- 2/3 cup water
- 1/4 cup olive oil
- 1 cup fresh tomatoes, diced
- 1 cup bell peppers, thinly sliced
- 1 cup red onions, finely chopped
- 1 cup shredded mozzarella cheese
- 1/2 cup crumbled feta cheese
- 2 cloves garlic, minced
- 1 teaspoon dried oregano
- Fresh basil leaves for garnish

Instructions:
1. Preheat and Prepare:
- Preheat your oven to 425°F (220°C).
- In a large mixing bowl, combine the all-purpose flour, baking powder, and salt.
2. Create Dough:
- Gradually add water and olive oil to the dry ingredients, mixing well until a soft dough forms.
- Knead the dough on a floured surface for about 5 minutes, or until it becomes smooth and elastic.
3. Roll Out the Flatbread:
- Divide the dough in half. Roll out each portion into a thin, rustic flatbread shape.
- Place the flatbreads on a baking sheet lined with parchment paper.
4. Prepare Toppings:
- In a bowl, mix together diced tomatoes, sliced bell peppers, chopped red onions, minced garlic, and dried oregano.
- Spread the vegetable mixture evenly over each flatbread.
5. Add Cheese:
- Sprinkle shredded mozzarella and crumbled feta cheese over the vegetable mixture.
6. Bake:
- Bake in the preheated oven for 15-20 minutes, or until the edges are golden brown, and the cheese is melted and bubbly.
7. Garnish and Serve:

- Remove from the oven and let it cool for a few minutes. Garnish with fresh basil leaves.
- Slice and serve the Farmstead Flatbread, capturing the essence of the bountiful yet straightforward meals found on the farmsteads of Steinbeck's narrative.

Nutrition Information:
Note: Nutritional values are approximate and may vary based on specific ingredients used.
- Calories per serving: 300
- Total Fat: 14g
- Saturated Fat: 5g
- Cholesterol: 20mg
- Sodium: 400mg
- Total Carbohydrates: 35g
- Dietary Fiber: 3g
- Sugars: 3g
- Protein: 10g

Enjoy this Farmstead Flatbread that embodies the spirit of resilience and simplicity inspired by "The Grapes of Wrath."

62. Hooverville Hotcakes

In the dust bowl era chronicled in John Steinbeck's iconic novel "The Grapes of Wrath," food often became a symbol of resilience and survival. One such dish that emerged from the hardships of the time is the "Hooverville Hotcakes." Named after the makeshift communities known as "Hoovervilles," these hotcakes reflect the resourcefulness and creativity of people during a challenging period in American history. Simple yet hearty, these hotcakes are a testament to the power of community and the ability to find comfort in even the most trying circumstances.

Serving: Makes approximately 8-10 hotcakes.
Preparation Time: 15 minutes
Ready Time: 30 minutes

Ingredients:

- 1 cup all-purpose flour
- 1 tablespoon sugar
- 1 teaspoon baking powder
- 1/2 teaspoon baking soda
- 1/4 teaspoon salt
- 1 cup buttermilk
- 1 large egg
- 2 tablespoons melted butter
- 1 teaspoon vanilla extract
- Cooking oil or butter for greasing the pan

Instructions:

1. In a large mixing bowl, whisk together the flour, sugar, baking powder, baking soda, and salt.

2. In a separate bowl, whisk together the buttermilk, egg, melted butter, and vanilla extract.

3. Pour the wet ingredients into the dry ingredients and stir until just combined. Do not overmix; a few lumps are okay.

4. Heat a griddle or non-stick skillet over medium heat and lightly grease with cooking oil or butter.

5. Using a ladle or measuring cup, pour about 1/4 cup of batter onto the griddle for each hotcake. Cook until bubbles form on the surface, then flip and cook until the other side is golden brown.

6. Repeat until all the batter is used, keeping the cooked hotcakes warm in a low oven if needed.

7. Serve the Hooverville Hotcakes with your favorite toppings, such as maple syrup, fresh fruit, or whipped cream.

Nutrition Information:

(Per serving, based on 2 hotcakes)
- Calories: 220
- Total Fat: 8g
- Saturated Fat: 4g
- Trans Fat: 0g
- Cholesterol: 50mg
- Sodium: 450mg
- Total Carbohydrates: 30g
- Dietary Fiber: 1g
- Sugars: 6g
- Protein: 6g

Note: Nutrition information is approximate and may vary based on specific ingredients and serving sizes.

63. Depression Delight Delicata Squash

In the arduous journey chronicled in John Steinbeck's "The Grapes of Wrath," where despair and resilience coexist, we draw inspiration for our "Depression Delight Delicata Squash." This dish pays homage to the endurance of the human spirit, much like the Joad family's tenacity in the face of adversity. Delicata squash, with its sweet and nutty flavor, becomes a symbol of sustenance during challenging times. Let this Depression Delight bring warmth and comfort to your table, echoing the strength found within the pages of Steinbeck's timeless narrative.

Serving: 4 servings
Preparation Time: 15 minutes
Ready Time: 45 minutes

Ingredients:
- 2 medium-sized Delicata squash
- 2 tablespoons olive oil
- 1 teaspoon dried thyme
- 1 teaspoon smoked paprika
- Salt and pepper to taste
- 1 cup quinoa
- 2 cups vegetable broth
- 1/2 cup chopped walnuts
- 1/4 cup dried cranberries
- 1/4 cup crumbled feta cheese (optional)
- Fresh parsley for garnish

Instructions:
1. Preheat Oven: Preheat your oven to 400°F (200°C).
2. Prepare Squash: Wash the Delicata squash, cut them in half lengthwise, and scoop out the seeds. Slice the squash into half-moons, about 1/2 inch thick.
3. Season Squash: In a large bowl, toss the squash slices with olive oil, dried thyme, smoked paprika, salt, and pepper until evenly coated.

4. Roast Squash: Spread the seasoned squash on a baking sheet in a single layer. Roast in the preheated oven for 25-30 minutes or until the squash is tender and slightly caramelized, turning once halfway through.

5. Cook Quinoa: While the squash is roasting, rinse the quinoa under cold water. In a saucepan, combine quinoa and vegetable broth. Bring to a boil, then reduce heat, cover, and simmer for 15-20 minutes, or until the quinoa is cooked and the liquid is absorbed.

6. Combine Ingredients: In a large bowl, mix the cooked quinoa, roasted squash, chopped walnuts, and dried cranberries. If desired, sprinkle with crumbled feta cheese.

7. Garnish and Serve: Garnish the Depression Delight with fresh parsley. Serve warm, embracing the comforting flavors reminiscent of resilience and hope.

Nutrition Information:
Note: Nutrition information may vary based on optional ingredients and serving sizes.
- Calories: 350 per serving
- Protein: 9g
- Carbohydrates: 50g
- Dietary Fiber: 7g
- Sugars: 8g
- Fat: 14g
- Saturated Fat: 2g
- Cholesterol: 5mg
- Sodium: 450mg
- Vitamin D: 0%
- Calcium: 8%
- Iron: 20%
- Potassium: 620mg

64. Tractor Trail Mix

Step back in time and journey through the flavors of the Dust Bowl with our rustic and hearty "Tractor Trail Mix," inspired by John Steinbeck's classic novel, The Grapes of Wrath. This trail mix pays homage to the resilience of the Joad family as they faced the challenges of the Great Depression. Packed with a blend of wholesome ingredients, it's a snack that fuels both body and spirit. Take a bite and experience the essence of survival and perseverance.

Serving: Ideal for sharing, this recipe serves 8.
Preparation Time: 15 minutes
Ready Time: 15 minutes

Ingredients:
- 1 cup roasted almonds
- 1 cup dried cranberries
- 1 cup pumpkin seeds
- 1 cup sunflower seeds
- 1 cup whole-grain pretzels, broken into pieces
- 1 cup dried apple slices
- 1/2 cup dark chocolate chips
- 1/2 cup raisins
- 1/2 cup dried apricots, chopped

Instructions:
1. In a large mixing bowl, combine the roasted almonds, dried cranberries, pumpkin seeds, sunflower seeds, pretzels, dried apple slices, dark chocolate chips, raisins, and chopped dried apricots.
2. Gently toss the ingredients together until well mixed, ensuring an even distribution of flavors.
3. Transfer the trail mix to an airtight container, preserving its freshness and allowing the flavors to meld.
4. Serve in individual portions or enjoy as a communal snack during your literary gatherings or outdoor adventures.

Nutrition Information:
Note: Nutrition values are approximate and may vary based on specific ingredients used.
- Serving Size: 1/2 cup
- Calories: 220
- Total Fat: 12g
- Saturated Fat: 3g
- Trans Fat: 0g
- Cholesterol: 0mg
- Sodium: 120mg
- Total Carbohydrates: 25g

- Dietary Fiber: 4g
- Sugars: 12g
- Protein: 6g

Embrace the spirit of The Grapes of Wrath with this Tractor Trail Mix, a snack that embodies the resilience and strength of the human spirit. Perfect for literary gatherings or as a companion during your own journey, this trail mix is a flavorful homage to Steinbeck's enduring classic.

65. Corn Husk Wraps

In the spirit of John Steinbeck's "The Grapes of Wrath," where the Joad family faced adversity with resilience and resourcefulness, we present a humble yet delicious recipe inspired by the agricultural landscape of the novel. These Corn Husk Wraps pay homage to the simplicity and ingenuity found in the characters' journey, utilizing corn husks – a staple of the American Midwest.

Serving: Makes approximately 12 wraps
Preparation Time: 30 minutes
Ready Time: 1 hour

Ingredients:
- 2 cups masa harina (corn flour)
- 1 1/4 cups warm water
- 1/3 cup vegetable oil
- 1/2 teaspoon salt
- 1 cup cooked black beans
- 1 cup corn kernels (fresh or frozen)
- 1 cup diced tomatoes
- 1/2 cup diced red onion
- 1/4 cup chopped fresh cilantro
- 1 teaspoon ground cumin
- 1 teaspoon chili powder
- Salt and pepper to taste
- 12 corn husks, soaked in warm water for 30 minutes

Instructions:

1. In a large mixing bowl, combine masa harina, warm water, vegetable oil, and salt. Knead the mixture until it forms a smooth, pliable dough. If the dough is too dry, add a little more water; if too wet, add a bit more masa harina.

2. In a separate bowl, mix together the black beans, corn, tomatoes, red onion, cilantro, cumin, chili powder, salt, and pepper. Set aside.

3. Take a soaked corn husk and place a small amount of the masa harina dough in the center. Using your fingers, spread the dough evenly over the husk, leaving a border around the edges.

4. Spoon a generous amount of the bean and vegetable mixture onto the center of the dough-covered husk.

5. Fold the sides of the corn husk over the filling, creating a rectangular shape. Fold the top and bottom edges to seal the wrap.

6. Repeat the process with the remaining husks and filling.

7. Steam the wraps in a steamer basket for approximately 45 minutes to 1 hour, or until the masa harina is cooked through and the filling is heated.

8. Allow the wraps to cool for a few minutes before serving.

Nutrition Information:
(Per serving, based on 1 wrap)
- Calories: 180
- Total Fat: 6g
- Saturated Fat: 1g
- Cholesterol: 0mg
- Sodium: 200mg
- Total Carbohydrates: 28g
- Dietary Fiber: 5g
- Sugars: 2g
- Protein: 5g

These Corn Husk Wraps are a flavorful nod to the resilience of those who weathered the Dust Bowl era, bringing a taste of sustenance inspired by the indomitable spirit of Steinbeck's characters. Serve them with a side of history and a dollop of hope.

66. Breadline Bruschetta

As we delve into the culinary world inspired by John Steinbeck's iconic novel, "The Grapes of Wrath," we find ourselves drawn to the essence of resilience and simplicity reflected in the lives of the Joad family. In this homage to their journey, we present the "Breadline Bruschetta," a humble yet flavorful dish that pays tribute to the strength found in the face of adversity.

Serving: 4 servings
Preparation Time: 15 minutes
Ready Time: 20 minutes

Ingredients:
- 1 loaf of rustic Italian bread
- 4 large tomatoes, diced
- 1/2 red onion, finely chopped
- 2 cloves garlic, minced
- 1/4 cup fresh basil, chopped
- 1/4 cup extra-virgin olive oil
- 1 tablespoon balsamic vinegar
- Salt and pepper to taste
- 1/2 cup grated Parmesan cheese

Instructions:
1. Prepare the Bread: Preheat the oven to 375°F (190°C). Slice the Italian bread into 1/2-inch thick slices and place them on a baking sheet. Toast in the oven for about 5 minutes, or until the edges become golden brown.
2. Mix the Tomatoes: In a bowl, combine the diced tomatoes, red onion, minced garlic, and chopped basil. Drizzle the balsamic vinegar and olive oil over the mixture. Add salt and pepper to taste, then toss the ingredients until well combined.
3. Top the Bread: Remove the toasted bread from the oven and let it cool slightly. Spoon the tomato mixture generously over each slice of bread.
4. Finish with Parmesan: Sprinkle the grated Parmesan cheese evenly over the bruschetta.
5. Final Touch: Place the topped slices back in the oven for an additional 5 minutes, or until the cheese is melted and bubbly.
6. Serve: Arrange the Breadline Bruschetta on a platter and serve warm. This dish captures the essence of simple, wholesome ingredients—much like the meals cherished by the Joad family during their arduous journey.

Nutrition Information:
(Per Serving)
- Calories: 280
- Total Fat: 14g
- Saturated Fat: 3g
- Trans Fat: 0g
- Cholesterol: 7mg
- Sodium: 420mg
- Total Carbohydrates: 32g
- Dietary Fiber: 3g
- Sugars: 4g
- Protein: 9g
Note: Nutrition information is approximate and may vary based on specific ingredients used.

67. Sorghum Scones

In the heart of John Steinbeck's literary masterpiece, "The Grapes of Wrath," the Joad family embarks on a journey filled with hardship and resilience. Inspired by the themes of sustenance and endurance, these Sorghum Scones pay homage to the simple yet vital sustenance that kept the Joads moving forward. Sorghum, a hearty and nutritious grain, forms the backbone of these scones, offering a taste that resonates with the spirit of survival ingrained in Steinbeck's iconic tale.

Serving: Makes 12 scones
Preparation Time: 15 minutes
Ready Time: 30 minutes

Ingredients:
- 2 cups sorghum flour
- 1/4 cup sugar
- 1 tablespoon baking powder
- 1/2 teaspoon baking soda
- 1/2 teaspoon salt
- 1/2 cup unsalted butter, cold and cubed
- 1/2 cup buttermilk
- 1 large egg

- 1 teaspoon vanilla extract
- 1/2 cup raisins or currants (optional)
- 1 tablespoon milk (for brushing the tops)

Instructions:
1. Preheat the oven to 425°F (220°C) and line a baking sheet with parchment paper.
2. In a large mixing bowl, whisk together the sorghum flour, sugar, baking powder, baking soda, and salt.
3. Add the cold, cubed butter to the dry ingredients. Using a pastry cutter or your fingertips, work the butter into the flour mixture until it resembles coarse crumbs.
4. In a separate bowl, whisk together the buttermilk, egg, and vanilla extract.
5. Pour the wet ingredients into the dry ingredients and gently stir until just combined. If desired, fold in raisins or currants.
6. Turn the dough out onto a lightly floured surface and knead it a few times until it comes together. Pat the dough into a circle about 1 inch thick.
7. Using a sharp knife or a round cutter, cut the dough into 12 wedges or rounds.
8. Place the scones on the prepared baking sheet, leaving some space between each.
9. Brush the tops of the scones with a little milk to give them a golden finish.
10. Bake in the preheated oven for 12-15 minutes or until the edges are golden brown.
11. Allow the scones to cool on a wire rack for a few minutes before serving.

Nutrition Information:
(Per serving, based on 12 servings)
- Calories: 180
- Total Fat: 8g
- Saturated Fat: 5g
- Cholesterol: 35mg
- Sodium: 290mg
- Total Carbohydrates: 25g
- Dietary Fiber: 2g
- Sugars: 6g

- Protein: 3g

These Sorghum Scones are a testament to the strength found in simplicity, mirroring the resilience of the Joad family as they faced the challenges of their journey. Enjoy a taste of history and literary inspiration with each bite.

68. Apple Orchard Amaretto

Embark on a culinary journey inspired by John Steinbeck's classic novel, "The Grapes of Wrath," with our delightful recipe for "Apple Orchard Amaretto." This dish pays homage to the abundance of flavors found in the bountiful orchards and the resilient spirit of those facing adversity. The combination of crisp apples and the sweet essence of amaretto creates a symphony of taste that will transport you to the heart of an apple orchard in full bloom.

Serving: 4 servings
Preparation Time: 15 minutes
Ready Time: 45 minutes

Ingredients:
- 4 large apples, peeled, cored, and thinly sliced (use a variety like Honeycrisp or Granny Smith)
- 1/2 cup brown sugar, packed
- 1/4 cup unsalted butter, melted
- 1/4 cup amaretto liqueur
- 1 teaspoon ground cinnamon
- 1/4 teaspoon nutmeg, freshly grated
- 1/2 cup old-fashioned rolled oats
- 1/3 cup all-purpose flour
- 1/4 cup sliced almonds
- Vanilla ice cream or whipped cream for serving (optional)

Instructions:
1. Preheat Oven:
Preheat your oven to 350°F (175°C).
2. Prepare Apples:
Peel, core, and thinly slice the apples. Place them in a large mixing bowl.

3. Amaretto Mixture:
In a separate bowl, mix together the melted butter, brown sugar, amaretto liqueur, ground cinnamon, and freshly grated nutmeg.
4. Coat Apples:
Pour the amaretto mixture over the sliced apples and toss until the apples are evenly coated.
5. Layer in Baking Dish:
Transfer the coated apples to a greased baking dish, spreading them out evenly.
6. Oat Topping:
In a mixing bowl, combine the rolled oats, all-purpose flour, and sliced almonds. Sprinkle this mixture over the apples, creating a crumbly topping.
7. Bake:
Place the baking dish in the preheated oven and bake for 30-35 minutes or until the topping is golden brown, and the apples are tender.
8. Serve:
Allow the Apple Orchard Amaretto to cool for a few minutes before serving. Optionally, serve with a scoop of vanilla ice cream or a dollop of whipped cream for an extra indulgence.

Nutrition Information:
(Per serving)
- Calories: 280
- Total Fat: 11g
- Saturated Fat: 6g
- Trans Fat: 0g
- Cholesterol: 25mg
- Sodium: 10mg
- Total Carbohydrates: 42g
- Dietary Fiber: 5g
- Sugars: 30g
- Protein: 2g
Indulge in the comforting warmth of Apple Orchard Amaretto, a dish that captures the essence of resilience and the simple joys found even in the face of hardship.

69. Route 66 Roasted Radishes

Embark on a culinary journey inspired by John Steinbeck's masterpiece, "The Grapes of Wrath," and explore the flavors of the iconic Route 66. These Roasted Radishes pay homage to the resilient spirit of the characters as they traversed the historic highway during challenging times. Roasting radishes transforms their peppery bite into a caramelized sweetness, creating a simple yet delightful dish that captures the essence of the journey.

Serving: 4 servings
Preparation Time: 15 minutes
Ready Time: 40 minutes

Ingredients:
- 2 bunches of fresh radishes, washed and trimmed
- 2 tablespoons olive oil
- 1 teaspoon dried thyme
- 1 teaspoon garlic powder
- Salt and pepper to taste
- 1 tablespoon fresh parsley, chopped (for garnish)

Instructions:
1. Preheat your oven to 400°F (200°C).
2. Halve or quarter the radishes depending on their size, ensuring uniform pieces for even roasting.
3. In a large mixing bowl, toss the radishes with olive oil, dried thyme, garlic powder, salt, and pepper, ensuring they are well coated.
4. Spread the seasoned radishes in a single layer on a baking sheet.
5. Roast in the preheated oven for approximately 25-30 minutes or until the radishes are golden brown and tender, stirring once halfway through.
6. Remove from the oven and transfer the roasted radishes to a serving dish.
7. Garnish with fresh chopped parsley for a burst of color and added freshness.
8. Serve warm as a side dish, allowing the flavors to transport you to the historic Route 66.

Nutrition Information:
(Per Serving)

- Calories: 85
- Total Fat: 7g
- Saturated Fat: 1g
- Cholesterol: 0mg
- Sodium: 78mg
- Total Carbohydrates: 5g
- Dietary Fiber: 2g
- Sugars: 2g
- Protein: 1g

Delight in the simplicity of Route 66 Roasted Radishes, a dish that echoes the resilience and strength found along the journey of "The Grapes of Wrath."

70. Migrant Mushroom Mousse

In homage to John Steinbeck's iconic novel, "The Grapes of Wrath," we present the "Migrant Mushroom Mousse." This dish is a culinary reflection of the struggles and resilience depicted in the novel, capturing the essence of migration and the beauty that can arise from challenging circumstances. The rich, earthy flavors of mushrooms symbolize the perseverance and strength of the characters, creating a dish that is both flavorful and evocative.

Serving: 4 servings
Preparation Time: 15 minutes
Ready Time: 2 hours (including chilling time)

Ingredients:
- 1 pound fresh mushrooms (such as cremini or button), finely chopped
- 2 tablespoons olive oil
- 1 small onion, finely diced
- 2 cloves garlic, minced
- 1/4 cup dry white wine
- 1 teaspoon thyme leaves, chopped
- Salt and black pepper to taste
- 1 cup heavy cream
- 2 teaspoons gelatin powder
- 1/4 cup cold water

- Fresh chives for garnish

Instructions:

1. Sauté the Mushrooms:
- In a large skillet, heat olive oil over medium heat. Add the diced onions and garlic, sautéing until softened and fragrant.
- Add the chopped mushrooms and thyme to the skillet. Cook until the mushrooms release their moisture and become golden brown.
- Pour in the white wine, allowing it to reduce by half. Season with salt and pepper to taste. Remove from heat and let it cool slightly.
2. Prepare the Gelatin:
- In a small bowl, sprinkle gelatin over cold water. Let it sit for a few minutes to bloom.
3. Blend the Mushroom Mixture:
- Transfer the sautéed mushroom mixture to a blender. Blend until smooth.
4. Heat the Cream:
- In a saucepan, heat the heavy cream until it's warm but not boiling. Add the bloomed gelatin, stirring until fully dissolved.
5. Combine Mushroom Puree and Cream:
- Pour the warm cream mixture into the blender with the mushroom puree. Blend until well combined.
6. Chill the Mousse:
- Pour the mushroom mousse into individual serving dishes or a large serving dish. Refrigerate for at least 2 hours or until set.
7. Garnish and Serve:
- Before serving, garnish with fresh chives. This dish can be enjoyed on its own or with crusty bread.

Nutrition Information:
(Per Serving)
- Calories: 280
- Protein: 5g
- Carbohydrates: 6g
- Fat: 26g
- Saturated Fat: 15g
- Cholesterol: 80mg
- Sodium: 40mg
- Fiber: 1g
- Sugar: 2g

Note: Nutrition information is approximate and may vary based on specific ingredients used.

71. Oakie Oatcakes

In the heart of John Steinbeck's "The Grapes of Wrath," where hardship meets resilience, we draw inspiration for a humble yet sustaining dish: Oakie Oatcakes. These simple oatcakes embody the spirit of endurance and resourcefulness, echoing the struggles faced by the Joad family as they navigate the Dust Bowl era. Enjoy these nutritious and rustic oatcakes that pay homage to the enduring strength found within the pages of this literary classic.

Serving: 12 oatcakes
Preparation Time: 15 minutes
Ready Time: 30 minutes

Ingredients:
- 2 cups rolled oats
- 1 cup whole wheat flour
- 1 teaspoon baking powder
- 1/2 teaspoon baking soda
- 1/2 teaspoon salt
- 1/4 cup unsalted butter, cold and cubed
- 1 cup buttermilk
- 2 tablespoons honey
- 1 large egg

Instructions:
1. Preheat your oven to 375°F (190°C). Grease a baking sheet or line it with parchment paper.
2. In a large mixing bowl, combine the rolled oats, whole wheat flour, baking powder, baking soda, and salt.
3. Add the cold, cubed butter to the dry ingredients. Use your fingertips to rub the butter into the flour mixture until it resembles coarse crumbs.
4. In a separate bowl, whisk together the buttermilk, honey, and egg.
5. Pour the wet ingredients into the dry ingredients and stir until just combined. Be careful not to overmix; a slightly lumpy batter is okay.

6. Scoop 1/4 cup portions of the batter onto the prepared baking sheet, spacing them about 2 inches apart. Use the back of a spoon to slightly flatten and shape each oatcake.
7. Bake in the preheated oven for 15-18 minutes or until the edges are golden brown.
8. Allow the Oakie Oatcakes to cool on the baking sheet for a few minutes before transferring them to a wire rack to cool completely.

Nutrition Information (per oatcake):
- Calories: 120
- Total Fat: 4g
- Saturated Fat: 2g
- Cholesterol: 20mg
- Sodium: 220mg
- Total Carbohydrates: 19g
- Dietary Fiber: 2g
- Sugars: 4g
- Protein: 4g

Embrace the nourishing simplicity of Oakie Oatcakes—a tribute to the indomitable spirit of those who weathered the storm in Steinbeck's masterpiece. These hearty oatcakes serve as a reminder that even in the harshest of times, sustenance and strength can be found in the most basic of ingredients.

72. Jicama Julep

In the heart of John Steinbeck's iconic novel, "The Grapes of Wrath," lies a tale of resilience, survival, and the pursuit of the American dream. Inspired by the themes of sustenance and endurance, we present the "Jicama Julep," a refreshing dish that echoes the strength and determination of the characters in Steinbeck's masterpiece. This delightful recipe brings together the crispness of jicama with a minty twist, offering a taste of hope and renewal.

Serving: 4 servings
Preparation Time: 15 minutes
Ready Time: 15 minutes

Ingredients:
- 1 large jicama, peeled and julienned
- 1 cup fresh mint leaves, finely chopped
- 1/2 cup simple syrup
- 1/4 cup fresh lime juice
- 2 cups crushed ice
- 1 cup sparkling water
- Mint sprigs for garnish
- Lime slices for garnish

Instructions:
1. Prepare the Jicama:
- Peel the jicama and cut it into thin, matchstick-like julienne strips. Set aside.
2. Mint Simple Syrup:
- In a small saucepan, combine the chopped mint and simple syrup over medium heat. Stir until the mixture simmers, then remove from heat. Allow it to cool and strain out the mint leaves.
3. Mixing the Jicama Julep:
- In a large bowl, combine the julienned jicama, lime juice, and the mint-infused simple syrup. Toss the ingredients together until the jicama is well-coated.
4. Assembling the Julep:
- Fill serving glasses with crushed ice. Spoon the jicama mixture over the ice, distributing it evenly.
5. Adding Sparkle:
- Pour sparkling water over each glass, allowing the effervescence to mingle with the jicama and mint flavors.
6. Garnish:
- Garnish each glass with a mint sprig and a slice of lime for a burst of color and added freshness.
7. Serve:
- Serve the Jicama Julep immediately, allowing the cool and invigorating flavors to transport you to the dusty roads and hopeful horizons of Steinbeck's epic tale.

Nutrition Information:
(Per Serving)
- Calories: 90
- Total Fat: 0g

- Cholesterol: 0mg
- Sodium: 10mg
- Total Carbohydrates: 23g
- Dietary Fiber: 7g
- Sugars: 12g
- Protein: 1g

Note: Nutrition information is approximate and may vary based on specific ingredients and portion sizes.

73. Grapevine Gazpacho

Step into the dusty, sun-soaked fields of the Joad family's journey in "The Grapes of Wrath" with this refreshing Grapevine Gazpacho. Inspired by the resilience of the characters in Steinbeck's classic novel, this chilled soup captures the essence of the California vineyards and the simplicity of farm life. Bursting with flavors of ripe tomatoes, crisp cucumbers, and the sweetness of grapes, this Grapevine Gazpacho is a celebration of the bountiful harvest amid challenging times.

Serving: 4 servings
Preparation Time: 15 minutes
Ready Time: 2 hours (including chilling time)

Ingredients:
- 4 large tomatoes, diced
- 1 cucumber, peeled and diced
- 1 red bell pepper, diced
- 1 cup red grapes, halved
- 1/2 red onion, finely chopped
- 2 cloves garlic, minced
- 4 cups tomato juice
- 1/4 cup red wine vinegar
- 1/4 cup extra-virgin olive oil
- 1 teaspoon sugar
- Salt and pepper to taste
- Fresh basil leaves for garnish

Instructions:

1. In a large mixing bowl, combine the diced tomatoes, cucumber, red bell pepper, grapes, red onion, and minced garlic.
2. In a separate bowl, whisk together the tomato juice, red wine vinegar, olive oil, sugar, salt, and pepper until well combined.
3. Pour the liquid mixture over the chopped vegetables and stir gently to combine. Adjust the seasoning according to your taste.
4. Cover the bowl and refrigerate the gazpacho for at least 2 hours to allow the flavors to meld and the soup to chill.
5. Before serving, give the gazpacho a final stir. Ladle the chilled soup into bowls.
6. Garnish each serving with fresh basil leaves for a burst of aromatic flavor.

Nutrition Information:
(per serving)
- Calories: 180
- Total Fat: 12g
- Saturated Fat: 2g
- Cholesterol: 0mg
- Sodium: 420mg
- Total Carbohydrates: 18g
- Dietary Fiber: 4g
- Sugars: 10g
- Protein: 3g
Celebrate the harvest of the land with this Grapevine Gazpacho, a tribute to the enduring spirit of the Joads and the rich agricultural heritage depicted in "The Grapes of Wrath."

74. Tomato Tin Tamales

Inspired by the hardships and resilience portrayed in John Steinbeck's "The Grapes of Wrath," these Tomato Tin Tamales pay homage to the resourcefulness of those facing adversity. In the spirit of making the most of simple ingredients, this recipe transforms canned tomatoes into a delightful and comforting dish that reflects the strength found in times of struggle.

Serving: Makes approximately 12 tamales.

Preparation Time: 30 minutes
Ready Time: 1 hour 30 minutes

Ingredients:
- 2 cups masa harina
- 1 cup vegetable broth
- 1/2 cup vegetable oil
- 1 teaspoon baking powder
- 1/2 teaspoon salt
- 1 can (14 ounces) diced tomatoes, drained
- 1 cup corn kernels (fresh or frozen)
- 1 cup black beans, cooked and mashed
- 1 teaspoon ground cumin
- 1 teaspoon chili powder
- 1/2 cup chopped cilantro
- 12 corn husks, soaked in warm water until pliable

Instructions:
1. Prepare the Masa Dough: In a large bowl, combine masa harina, vegetable broth, vegetable oil, baking powder, and salt. Mix until you have a smooth, pliable dough.
2. Make the Filling: In another bowl, mix the drained diced tomatoes, corn kernels, mashed black beans, cumin, chili powder, and chopped cilantro. This will be your tamale filling.
3. Assemble the Tamales: Take a soaked corn husk and spread a thin layer of masa dough on it, leaving space at the edges. Spoon a generous tablespoon of the filling down the center of the dough.
4. Fold and Tie: Fold the sides of the husk over the filling, sealing the dough. Tie the tamale with a strip of soaked corn husk to secure it.
5. Steam the Tamales: Arrange the tamales in a steamer, standing them upright. Steam for about 1 hour until the masa is cooked through and firm.
6. Serve: Allow the tamales to cool for a few minutes before serving. Serve with your favorite salsa or a dollop of sour cream.

Nutrition Information:
Note: Nutritional values are approximate and may vary based on specific ingredients used.
- Calories per serving: 180
- Total Fat: 8g

- Saturated Fat: 1g
- Cholesterol: 0mg
- Sodium: 220mg
- Total Carbohydrates: 25g
- Dietary Fiber: 4g
- Sugars: 2g
- Protein: 4g

These Tomato Tin Tamales celebrate the ability to create something delicious and meaningful with simple, readily available ingredients, echoing the resilience and creativity found in the pages of "The Grapes of Wrath." Enjoy this taste of resourcefulness and community.

75. Dust Bowl Date Nut Bread

As we delve into the culinary world inspired by John Steinbeck's timeless classic, "The Grapes of Wrath," we stumble upon a recipe that pays homage to the resilience and resourcefulness of those who endured the Dust Bowl era. The Dust Bowl Date Nut Bread embodies the spirit of making do with what little was available during those challenging times. This hearty bread, rich with dates and nuts, serves as a testament to the strength found in simplicity.

Serving: 12 slices
Preparation Time: 15 minutes
Ready Time: 1 hour and 15 minutes

Ingredients:
- 1 cup chopped dates
- 1 cup boiling water
- 1 teaspoon baking soda
- 2 tablespoons unsalted butter, softened
- 1 cup granulated sugar
- 1 large egg, beaten
- 1 teaspoon vanilla extract
- 1 1/2 cups all-purpose flour
- 1 teaspoon baking powder
- 1/2 teaspoon salt
- 1 cup chopped nuts (walnuts or pecans work well)

Instructions:
1. Preheat your oven to 350°F (175°C). Grease and flour a 9x5-inch loaf pan.
2. In a bowl, combine the chopped dates and baking soda. Pour the boiling water over the dates and let them soak for 5-7 minutes until softened. Once softened, drain the excess water and set aside.
3. In a large mixing bowl, cream together the softened butter and sugar until light and fluffy.
4. Add the beaten egg and vanilla extract to the butter-sugar mixture. Mix well.
5. In a separate bowl, whisk together the flour, baking powder, and salt.
6. Gradually add the dry ingredients to the wet ingredients, mixing until just combined.
7. Fold in the chopped dates and nuts into the batter until evenly distributed.
8. Pour the batter into the prepared loaf pan and smooth the top.
9. Bake in the preheated oven for approximately 1 hour, or until a toothpick inserted into the center comes out clean.
10. Allow the Dust Bowl Date Nut Bread to cool in the pan for 10 minutes before transferring it to a wire rack to cool completely.

Nutrition Information:
(Per serving)
- Calories: 250
- Total Fat: 10g
- Saturated Fat: 3g
- Trans Fat: 0g
- Cholesterol: 25mg
- Sodium: 200mg
- Total Carbohydrates: 38g
- Dietary Fiber: 2g
- Sugars: 22g
- Protein: 4g

This Dust Bowl Date Nut Bread is a flavorful journey back in time, capturing the essence of survival and making something delicious out of the humblest ingredients. Enjoy a slice of history with this wholesome and comforting bread.

76. Okie Olive Tapenade

In John Steinbeck's "The Grapes of Wrath," the Joad family embarks on a journey through the Dust Bowl, facing hardship but also finding moments of resilience and resourcefulness. Inspired by this tale, the Okie Olive Tapenade captures the essence of the journey—simple, flavorful, and made from the available resources of the time. This zesty tapenade pays homage to the resilience and ingenuity of the characters, bringing together bold flavors reminiscent of the arduous journey.

Serving: Makes approximately 1 ½ cups of tapenade, serving 6-8 people.
Preparation Time: 15 minutes
Ready Time: 15 minutes

Ingredients:
- 1 cup pitted black olives, drained
- 1 cup pitted green olives, drained
- 2 tablespoons capers, drained
- 3 cloves garlic, minced
- 2 anchovy fillets (optional, for added depth of flavor)
- 1 tablespoon fresh thyme leaves
- 2 tablespoons fresh parsley, chopped
- 1 tablespoon lemon zest
- 3 tablespoons lemon juice
- 1/4 cup extra-virgin olive oil
- Salt and pepper to taste

Instructions:
1. Prep Ingredients:
- Rinse and drain the olives and capers to remove excess brine.
- Finely chop the black and green olives separately. Keep a coarse texture for added appeal.
2. Mixing the Tapenade:
- In a food processor, combine the chopped black olives, green olives, capers, minced garlic, anchovy fillets (if using), thyme leaves, parsley, lemon zest, and lemon juice.
- Pulse the mixture until coarsely chopped and blended but not fully pureed.
3. Adding Olive Oil and Seasoning:

132

- While the food processor is running, gradually pour in the olive oil until the tapenade reaches a spreadable consistency.
- Season with salt and pepper to taste. Remember, the olives and capers might already add saltiness, so adjust accordingly.
4. Adjusting Consistency and Flavor:
- If needed, adjust the consistency by adding a touch more olive oil or lemon juice. Taste and adjust seasonings as per preference.
5. Serve or Store:
- Transfer the Okie Olive Tapenade to a bowl. It can be served immediately or refrigerated for later use.
- Before serving, allow it to sit at room temperature for 15-20 minutes to enhance the flavors.

Nutrition Information:
(Approximate values per serving, based on 1/4 cup serving)
- Calories: 110
- Total Fat: 11g
- Saturated Fat: 1.5g
- Sodium: 450mg
- Total Carbohydrates: 2g
- Dietary Fiber: 1g
- Sugars: 0g
- Protein: 1g
This Okie Olive Tapenade captures the essence of resourcefulness and resilience, offering a flavorful spread that pairs wonderfully with crusty bread, crackers, or as a condiment for various dishes—a humble yet robust tribute to the enduring spirit portrayed in Steinbeck's classic novel.

77. Route 66 Red Lentil Soup

Embark on a culinary journey reminiscent of the iconic novel "The Grapes of Wrath" by John Steinbeck with our "Route 66 Red Lentil Soup." This hearty and wholesome soup pays homage to the resilience and spirit of the Dust Bowl era, offering a taste of comfort that transcends time. With the rustic charm of Route 66, this red lentil soup is a nourishing bowl that warms both body and soul.

Serving: 6 servings
Preparation Time: 15 minutes
Ready Time: 45 minutes

Ingredients:
- 1 cup red lentils, rinsed and drained
- 1 large onion, finely chopped
- 3 cloves garlic, minced
- 2 carrots, diced
- 2 celery stalks, diced
- 1 can (14 oz) diced tomatoes
- 6 cups vegetable broth
- 1 teaspoon ground cumin
- 1 teaspoon ground coriander
- 1/2 teaspoon smoked paprika
- Salt and black pepper to taste
- 2 tablespoons olive oil
- Fresh cilantro or parsley for garnish

Instructions:
1. In a large pot, heat olive oil over medium heat. Add the chopped onions and garlic, sautéing until softened and fragrant.
2. Add carrots and celery to the pot, continuing to sauté for an additional 3-4 minutes until the vegetables begin to soften.
3. Stir in the ground cumin, ground coriander, smoked paprika, salt, and black pepper. Allow the spices to toast for about 1-2 minutes, enhancing their flavors.
4. Pour in the red lentils, diced tomatoes, and vegetable broth. Bring the mixture to a gentle boil, then reduce the heat to simmer. Cover the pot and let it cook for approximately 30-35 minutes, or until the lentils are tender.
5. Taste and adjust the seasoning if necessary. For a creamier consistency, you can use an immersion blender to partially blend the soup.
6. Serve hot, garnished with fresh cilantro or parsley.

Nutrition Information:
(Per Serving)
- Calories: 220 kcal
- Protein: 12g

- Fat: 5g
- Carbohydrates: 32g
- Fiber: 10g
- Sugars: 5g
- Sodium: 800mg

Delight in the flavors of a bygone era, as you savor each spoonful of this Route 66 Red Lentil Soup—a culinary tribute to the enduring strength depicted in Steinbeck's masterpiece.

78. Vineyard Vodka Sauce

Embark on a culinary journey inspired by John Steinbeck's timeless masterpiece, "The Grapes of Wrath," with our delectable creation: Vineyard Vodka Sauce. This rich and savory sauce pays homage to the bountiful vineyards that grace the pages of Steinbeck's novel, bringing together the essence of the land and the warmth of family around the table.

Serving: 4-6 servings
Preparation Time: 15 minutes
Ready Time: 45 minutes

Ingredients:
- 2 tablespoons olive oil
- 1 onion, finely chopped
- 3 cloves garlic, minced
- 1/2 cup vodka
- 1 can (28 ounces) crushed tomatoes
- 1/2 cup heavy cream
- 1 teaspoon dried oregano
- 1 teaspoon dried basil
- 1/2 teaspoon red pepper flakes (optional)
- Salt and black pepper to taste
- 1/4 cup grated Parmesan cheese
- 1/4 cup fresh basil, chopped (for garnish)

Instructions:

1. Heat olive oil in a large saucepan over medium heat. Add chopped onions and sauté until translucent, about 5 minutes.
2. Add minced garlic to the onions and sauté for an additional 1-2 minutes until fragrant.
3. Pour in the vodka, and let it simmer for 2-3 minutes to allow the alcohol to evaporate.
4. Stir in the crushed tomatoes, oregano, basil, and red pepper flakes (if using). Season with salt and black pepper to taste.
5. Reduce the heat to low and let the sauce simmer for 30 minutes, allowing the flavors to meld.
6. Pour in the heavy cream, stirring to combine. Simmer for an additional 10 minutes, ensuring the sauce is heated through.
7. Stir in the grated Parmesan cheese until melted and well incorporated.
8. Remove the sauce from heat and let it rest for a few minutes before serving.
9. Garnish with fresh basil before serving.

Nutrition Information:
(Per serving - based on 4 servings)
- Calories: 320
- Total Fat: 18g
- Saturated Fat: 8g
- Cholesterol: 40mg
- Sodium: 620mg
- Total Carbohydrates: 28g
- Dietary Fiber: 6g
- Sugars: 15g
- Protein: 8g
Immerse yourself in the flavors of the vineyards with this Vineyard Vodka Sauce, a tribute to the resilience of the human spirit and the simple joys of sharing a meal with loved ones.

79. Peach Pit Pesto

Step into the rich tapestry of The Grapes of Wrath by John Steinbeck, where the Joad family embarks on a journey of survival and resilience during the Great Depression. Inspired by the spirit of resourcefulness and the bountiful harvests along the way, we present the Peach Pit

Pesto—an inventive creation rooted in the essence of the novel. Transforming humble peach pits into a flavorful pesto, this dish symbolizes the strength found in unexpected places.

Serving: 4 servings
Preparation Time: 15 minutes
Ready Time: 20 minutes

Ingredients:
- 2 cups peach pits, cleaned and dried
- 1 cup fresh basil leaves, packed
- 1/2 cup grated Parmesan cheese
- 1/2 cup toasted pine nuts
- 2 cloves garlic
- 1 cup extra-virgin olive oil
- Salt and pepper to taste

Instructions:
1. Prepare Peach Pits:
- Collect peach pits and thoroughly clean them.
- Dry the peach pits completely before use.
2. Toast Pine Nuts:
- In a dry skillet, toast the pine nuts over medium heat until golden brown. Stir frequently to prevent burning.
3. Blend Ingredients:
- In a food processor, combine peach pits, basil leaves, Parmesan cheese, toasted pine nuts, and garlic cloves.
- Pulse until the ingredients are finely chopped.
4. Stream in Olive Oil:
- With the food processor running, slowly stream in the olive oil until the pesto reaches a smooth consistency.
5. Season:
- Add salt and pepper to taste. Pulse again to incorporate the seasoning.
6. Adjust Consistency:
- If the pesto is too thick, add more olive oil until it reaches your desired consistency.
7. Serve:
- Spoon the Peach Pit Pesto over pasta, grilled vegetables, or as a spread on crusty bread.

Nutrition Information (per serving):
- Calories: 320
- Total Fat: 30g
- Saturated Fat: 5g
- Trans Fat: 0g
- Cholesterol: 10mg
- Sodium: 150mg
- Total Carbohydrates: 5g
- Dietary Fiber: 2g
- Sugars: 1g
- Protein: 7g

Embrace the inventive spirit of The Grapes of Wrath with this Peach Pit Pesto—a flavorful testament to resilience and creativity in the face of adversity.

80. Migrant Mango Chutney

As we journey through the culinary landscape inspired by John Steinbeck's timeless classic, "The Grapes of Wrath," we stumble upon the "Migrant Mango Chutney." This vibrant and flavorful condiment pays homage to the resilience of the Joad family and the migrants of their time, who faced hardships with a tenacious spirit. This chutney encapsulates the essence of the journey, combining sweet and savory flavors reminiscent of the diverse experiences woven into the novel.

Serving: Ideal for serving as a side dish or accompaniment, this Migrant Mango Chutney pairs perfectly with grilled meats, curries, or as a topping for your favorite crackers. It's a versatile addition to any meal, adding a burst of flavor that transports you to the heart of the Joad family's journey.
Preparation Time: 20 minutes
Ready Time: 1 hour (including cooling time)

Ingredients:
- 2 large ripe mangoes, peeled and diced
- 1 cup red onion, finely chopped
- 1 cup brown sugar
- 1 cup apple cider vinegar

- 1/2 cup raisins
- 1/4 cup crystallized ginger, finely chopped
- 1 teaspoon mustard seeds
- 1 teaspoon ground cinnamon
- 1/2 teaspoon ground cloves
- 1/2 teaspoon turmeric
- 1/2 teaspoon salt
- 1/4 teaspoon cayenne pepper (adjust to taste)

Instructions:

1. In a large saucepan, combine diced mangoes, chopped red onion, brown sugar, apple cider vinegar, raisins, crystallized ginger, mustard seeds, ground cinnamon, ground cloves, turmeric, salt, and cayenne pepper.
2. Bring the mixture to a boil over medium heat, stirring frequently to dissolve the sugar.
3. Once it reaches a boil, reduce the heat to low and simmer uncovered for about 45-50 minutes or until the chutney has thickened, and the mangoes are soft. Stir occasionally to prevent sticking.
4. Remove the saucepan from heat and let the chutney cool to room temperature. It will continue to thicken as it cools.
5. Transfer the Migrant Mango Chutney to sterilized jars and refrigerate. Allow it to chill for at least 30 minutes before serving.

Nutrition Information:

(Per 2-tablespoon serving)
- Calories: 60
- Total Fat: 0g
- Cholesterol: 0mg
- Sodium: 50mg
- Total Carbohydrates: 15g
- Dietary Fiber: 1g
- Sugars: 13g
- Protein: 0g

The Migrant Mango Chutney captures the essence of migration and endurance, making it a poignant addition to your culinary journey through the pages of "The Grapes of Wrath."

81. Weedpatch Walnut Waffles

'Weedpatch Walnut Waffles" pays homage to the resilience and resourcefulness of the Joad family in John Steinbeck's "The Grapes of Wrath." Inspired by the agricultural themes and the Joads' journey through the Dust Bowl, these waffles incorporate hearty walnuts, a staple ingredient found in many Depression-era recipes. The Weedpatch Camp, a government-managed camp for migrant workers, symbolizes hope and community, just like these comforting waffles aim to do. Enjoy a taste of history with this wholesome breakfast dish.

Serving: - Makes approximately 6-8 waffles.
Preparation Time: - 15 minutes
Ready Time: - 30 minutes

Ingredients:
- 2 cups all-purpose flour
- 2 tablespoons granulated sugar
- 1 tablespoon baking powder
- ½ teaspoon salt
- 2 large eggs, separated
- 1 ¾ cups milk
- ½ cup unsalted butter, melted and slightly cooled
- 1 teaspoon vanilla extract
- 1 cup chopped walnuts
- Cooking spray or additional butter for greasing the waffle iron

Instructions:
1. Preheat your waffle iron according to the manufacturer's instructions.
2. In a large mixing bowl, whisk together the flour, sugar, baking powder, and salt.
3. In another bowl, beat the egg whites until stiff peaks form. Set aside.
4. In a separate bowl, whisk together the egg yolks, milk, melted butter, and vanilla extract.
5. Pour the wet ingredients into the dry ingredients and mix until just combined. Fold in the chopped walnuts gently.
6. Carefully fold the beaten egg whites into the batter, maintaining a light and airy texture.
7. Lightly grease the waffle iron with cooking spray or butter.

8. Pour an appropriate amount of batter onto the preheated waffle iron and cook according to the manufacturer's instructions or until golden brown and crispy.

9. Once done, transfer the waffles to a plate and keep warm. Repeat with the remaining batter.

10. Serve the Weedpatch Walnut Waffles warm, topped with syrup, fresh fruit, whipped cream, or any desired toppings.

Nutrition Information (approximate values per serving):
- Calories: 350
- Total Fat: 20g
- Saturated Fat: 8g
- Trans Fat: 0g
- Cholesterol: 85mg
- Sodium: 480mg
- Total Carbohydrate: 35g
- Dietary Fiber: 2g
- Sugars: 6g
- Protein: 9g

Nutritional values are approximate and may vary based on specific ingredients used. Adjustments can be made for dietary preferences or restrictions. Enjoy these Weedpatch Walnut Waffles as a delightful nod to the themes and characters of Steinbeck's enduring novel.

82. Bank Note Barley Salad

The Grapes of Wrath by John Steinbeck resonates with a profound connection to the land and the struggle for survival during challenging times. "Bank Note Barley Salad" pays homage to the resilience of the Joad family and their journey, featuring a blend of hearty barley, vibrant vegetables, and savory flavors that evoke the spirit of endurance and hope.

Serving: Serves 4-6
Preparation Time: 20 minutes
Ready Time: 45 minutes

Ingredients:

- 1 cup pearl barley, rinsed
- 2 cups vegetable or chicken broth
- 1 red bell pepper, diced
- 1 yellow bell pepper, diced
- 1 cup cherry tomatoes, halved
- 1/2 red onion, finely chopped
- 1/3 cup chopped fresh parsley
- 1/4 cup chopped fresh basil
- 1/2 cup crumbled feta cheese (optional)
- 1/4 cup extra-virgin olive oil
- 2 tablespoons red wine vinegar
- Salt and pepper to taste

Instructions:
1. In a medium saucepan, bring the broth to a boil. Add the rinsed barley, reduce heat to low, cover, and simmer for 30-35 minutes or until barley is tender and liquid is absorbed. Remove from heat and let it cool to room temperature.
2. In a large mixing bowl, combine the cooked barley, diced bell peppers, cherry tomatoes, chopped red onion, parsley, and basil.
3. In a small bowl, whisk together the olive oil, red wine vinegar, salt, and pepper to create the dressing.
4. Drizzle the dressing over the barley and vegetable mixture. Toss gently to combine, ensuring the dressing coats all the ingredients evenly.
5. If desired, sprinkle crumbled feta cheese over the salad for an extra burst of flavor and creaminess.
6. Refrigerate the salad for at least 15-20 minutes before serving to allow the flavors to meld together.

Nutrition Information:
Note: Nutritional values are approximate and may vary depending on ingredients used.
- Serving size: 1/6 of recipe
- Calories: 250
- Total Fat: 11g
- Saturated Fat: 2g
- Cholesterol: 8mg
- Sodium: 250mg
- Total Carbohydrate: 32g
- Dietary Fiber: 6g

- Sugars: 3g
- Protein: 6g

The "Bank Note Barley Salad" stands as a testament to resourcefulness, combining simple ingredients into a nourishing and flavorful dish that speaks to the resilience found in hardship, echoing the enduring spirit portrayed in The Grapes of Wrath. Serve this salad as a side or a light main course, savoring its wholesome flavors that honor the indomitable human spirit.

83. Hooverville Hummus

In John Steinbeck's novel "The Grapes of Wrath," the harsh realities of the Great Depression are vividly portrayed, including the struggle for sustenance and the resilience found in simple yet hearty meals. Hooverville Hummus is a tribute to this period, combining humble ingredients to create a flavorful and nutritious dish that echoes the resourcefulness of the characters in the story.

Serving: Makes approximately 2 cups of hummus.
Preparation time: 15 minutes
Ready time: 15 minutes

Ingredients:
- 1 can (15 oz) chickpeas (garbanzo beans), drained and rinsed
- 3 tablespoons tahini
- 2 cloves garlic, minced
- 1/4 cup extra-virgin olive oil
- Juice of 1 lemon
- 1/2 teaspoon ground cumin
- 1/2 teaspoon paprika
- Salt and pepper to taste
- Optional toppings: extra olive oil, chopped parsley, or paprika for garnish

Instructions:
1. In a food processor, combine the drained and rinsed chickpeas, tahini, minced garlic, lemon juice, ground cumin, paprika, salt, and pepper.

2. Blend the ingredients while slowly adding the extra-virgin olive oil until the mixture becomes smooth and creamy. If the hummus is too thick, add a tablespoon of water at a time to reach the desired consistency.

3. Taste the hummus and adjust seasoning as needed, adding more salt, pepper, or lemon juice to suit your preference.

4. Once blended to your desired consistency and taste, transfer the hummus to a serving bowl.

5. If desired, drizzle a bit of extra-virgin olive oil over the top and sprinkle with chopped parsley or paprika for a decorative touch.

6. Serve the Hooverville Hummus with fresh vegetables, pita bread, or crackers.

Nutrition Information (per 2 tablespoons serving):
- Calories: 70
- Total Fat: 5g
- Saturated Fat: 0.5g
- Sodium: 80mg
- Total Carbohydrates: 5g
- Dietary Fiber: 1g
- Sugars: 0g
- Protein: 2g

Note: Nutrition Information is approximate and may vary based on specific ingredients used.

This Hooverville Hummus recipe encapsulates the spirit of making the most out of simple, accessible ingredients during challenging times, offering a delicious and nutritious spread reminiscent of the resilience found in Steinbeck's characters.

84. Oakie Onion Dip

Step back in time to the Dust Bowl era with this Oakie Onion Dip inspired by John Steinbeck's classic novel, "The Grapes of Wrath." This savory and comforting dip pays homage to the resilience of the Oakies as they faced adversity during the Great Depression. A perfect addition to your gathering, this dip brings together simple ingredients to create a flavor reminiscent of the strength and unity found in Steinbeck's timeless tale.

Serving: Ideal for a group of 6-8 people.
Preparation Time: 15 minutes
Ready Time: 30 minutes

Ingredients:
- 2 large onions, finely chopped
- 2 tablespoons olive oil
- 1 teaspoon Worcestershire sauce
- 1 cup mayonnaise
- 1 cup sour cream
- 1 teaspoon garlic powder
- 1 teaspoon onion powder
- Salt and pepper to taste
- Fresh chives, chopped (for garnish)

Instructions:
1. In a skillet over medium heat, sauté the finely chopped onions in olive oil until they become golden brown and caramelized. This should take about 10-12 minutes. Set aside to cool.
2. In a mixing bowl, combine the mayonnaise, sour cream, Worcestershire sauce, garlic powder, onion powder, salt, and pepper.
3. Once the caramelized onions have cooled, fold them into the mayonnaise and sour cream mixture, ensuring even distribution.
4. Cover the bowl and refrigerate the dip for at least 15 minutes to allow the flavors to meld.
5. Before serving, garnish the Oakie Onion Dip with freshly chopped chives for a burst of freshness.
6. Serve the dip with your choice of dippables, such as tortilla chips, fresh vegetable sticks, or crackers.

Nutrition Information:
(per serving - based on 8 servings)
- Calories: 280
- Total Fat: 25g
- Saturated Fat: 6g
- Cholesterol: 25mg
- Sodium: 300mg
- Total Carbohydrates: 8g
- Dietary Fiber: 1g

- Sugars: 4g
- Protein: 2g
Note: Nutrition information is approximate and may vary based on specific ingredients used. Adjust serving size accordingly.

85. Grilled Grape Leaves

Inspired by John Steinbeck's masterpiece, "The Grapes of Wrath," this recipe for Grilled Grape Leaves pays homage to the resilience and simplicity portrayed in the novel. Much like the Joad family's journey, these grilled grape leaves are a blend of hearty flavors and straightforward ingredients. Filled with a savory mixture, each bite is a journey through the essence of the story, capturing the spirit of survival and strength.

Serving: This recipe serves 4.
Preparation Time: 20 minutes
Ready Time: 45 minutes

Ingredients:
- 1 cup grape leaves, preserved in brine
- 1 cup cooked quinoa
- 1/2 cup crumbled feta cheese
- 1/4 cup pine nuts, toasted
- 2 tablespoons fresh dill, chopped
- 1 tablespoon olive oil
- 1 clove garlic, minced
- 1 teaspoon lemon zest
- Salt and pepper to taste
- Lemon wedges for serving

Instructions:
1. Prepare the Grape Leaves:
- Rinse the preserved grape leaves under cold water to remove excess brine.
- Blanch the grape leaves in boiling water for 2 minutes, then drain and set aside.
2. Prepare the Filling:

- In a mixing bowl, combine the cooked quinoa, crumbled feta, toasted pine nuts, chopped dill, olive oil, minced garlic, and lemon zest.
- Season the mixture with salt and pepper to taste, ensuring a well-balanced flavor.
3. Assemble the Grilled Grape Leaves:
- Lay out a grape leaf with the veiny side facing up.
- Place a spoonful of the quinoa mixture near the stem end of the leaf.
- Fold the sides of the leaf over the filling and roll it tightly, forming a compact parcel.
4. Grill the Grape Leaves:
- Preheat the grill to medium-high heat.
- Brush the stuffed grape leaves with olive oil and place them on the grill.
- Grill for 3-4 minutes per side, or until the leaves develop a slight char and the filling is heated through.
5. Serve:
- Arrange the grilled grape leaves on a serving platter.
- Garnish with additional dill and serve with lemon wedges on the side.

Nutrition Information:
Note: Nutrition information is per serving.
- Calories: 220
- Protein: 7g
- Fat: 14g
- Carbohydrates: 18g
- Fiber: 3g
- Sugar: 1g
- Sodium: 580mg
Embrace the flavors of "The Grapes of Wrath" with this Grilled Grape Leaves recipe—a dish that encapsulates the enduring spirit found within the pages of Steinbeck's classic novel.

86. Cucumber Canapés

In the spirit of John Steinbeck's timeless classic, "The Grapes of Wrath," we present a refreshing and simple recipe that pays homage to the humble ingredients often found on the dusty roads of the Joad family's journey. These Cucumber Canapés encapsulate the essence of resilience and simplicity, offering a delightful burst of flavors reminiscent of the struggle and triumph portrayed in Steinbeck's masterpiece.

Serving: Makes 20 canapés
Preparation Time: 15 minutes
Ready Time: 15 minutes

Ingredients:
- 2 large cucumbers, peeled and sliced into 1/4-inch rounds
- 1 cup cherry tomatoes, halved
- 1/2 cup feta cheese, crumbled
- 1/4 cup red onion, finely diced
- 2 tablespoons fresh dill, chopped
- 1 tablespoon olive oil
- 1 tablespoon balsamic glaze
- Salt and pepper to taste

Instructions:
1. Prepare the Cucumbers:
- Peel the cucumbers and slice them into 1/4-inch rounds.
2. Assemble the Base:
- Arrange the cucumber rounds on a serving platter.
3. Add the Toppings:
- Place a halved cherry tomato on each cucumber round.
- Sprinkle crumbled feta cheese over the tomatoes.
- Distribute finely diced red onion evenly across the canapés.
4. Garnish:
- Drizzle olive oil and balsamic glaze over the canapés.
- Sprinkle fresh dill over the top.
5. Season:
- Season with salt and pepper to taste.
6. Serve:
- Arrange the canapés on a platter and serve immediately.

Nutrition Information:
(Per serving - 2 canapés)
- Calories: 45
- Total Fat: 3g
- Saturated Fat: 1g
- Cholesterol: 5mg

- Sodium: 75mg
- Total Carbohydrates: 4g
- Dietary Fiber: 1g
- Sugars: 2g
- Protein: 2g

These Cucumber Canapés offer a light and vibrant tribute to the enduring spirit found in "The Grapes of Wrath." The crispness of cucumber, combined with the tang of feta and the sweetness of tomatoes, creates a delightful appetizer that captures the essence of Steinbeck's narrative. Enjoy these canapés as a symbol of simplicity and sustenance, much like the Joad family cherished on their arduous journey.

87. Tomato Tin Tabbouleh

Step into the world of "The Grapes of Wrath" by John Steinbeck with this flavorful and refreshing Tomato Tin Tabbouleh. Inspired by the resilience and resourcefulness of the characters in the novel, this dish combines the simplicity of ingredients with the rich symbolism of the tomato tin, embodying the spirit of making the best out of what's available. As the Joad family adapted to their circumstances, let this Tomato Tin Tabbouleh inspire you to savor the goodness of life even in challenging times.

Serving: 4 servings
Preparation Time: 20 minutes
Ready Time: 30 minutes

Ingredients:
- 1 cup bulgur wheat
- 1 ½ cups boiling water
- 1 can (14 oz) diced tomatoes, drained
- 1 cucumber, diced
- 1 cup fresh parsley, finely chopped
- ½ cup fresh mint, finely chopped
- 1/3 cup red onion, finely chopped
- ¼ cup olive oil
- 3 tablespoons lemon juice

- Salt and pepper to taste

Instructions:
1. Place the bulgur wheat in a large bowl and pour the boiling water over it. Cover the bowl and let it sit for about 15 minutes or until the bulgur is tender and has absorbed the water.
2. Fluff the bulgur with a fork and allow it to cool to room temperature.
3. In a separate large mixing bowl, combine the diced tomatoes, cucumber, parsley, mint, and red onion.
4. Add the cooled bulgur to the vegetable mixture, tossing gently to combine.
5. In a small bowl, whisk together the olive oil, lemon juice, salt, and pepper.
6. Drizzle the dressing over the tabbouleh and toss until all ingredients are well coated.
7. Allow the flavors to meld by refrigerating the tabbouleh for at least 10 minutes before serving.
8. Serve chilled and enjoy the vibrant flavors of this Tomato Tin Tabbouleh, a dish that captures the essence of adaptation and resilience.

Nutrition Information:
(Per serving)
- Calories: 240
- Total Fat: 10g
- Saturated Fat: 1.5g
- Cholesterol: 0mg
- Sodium: 250mg
- Total Carbohydrates: 35g
- Dietary Fiber: 8g
- Sugars: 4g
- Protein: 6g

Embrace the spirit of "The Grapes of Wrath" with this Tomato Tin Tabbouleh, a dish that speaks to the heart of making the most of what you have.

88. Depression-Era Eggplant Parmesan

During the Depression era, families faced unprecedented challenges, and meals had to be crafted with frugality and creativity. Inspired by the spirit of resilience portrayed in John Steinbeck's "The Grapes of Wrath," this Depression-Era Eggplant Parmesan is a testament to making the most of simple ingredients. This comforting dish reflects the resourcefulness of families during difficult times, turning humble ingredients into a satisfying and flavorful meal.

Serving: 4 servings
Preparation Time: 20 minutes
Ready Time: 1 hour

Ingredients:
- 1 large eggplant, sliced into 1/2-inch rounds
- 1 cup all-purpose flour
- 2 large eggs, beaten
- 2 cups breadcrumbs
- 1 teaspoon dried oregano
- 1 teaspoon dried basil
- Salt and black pepper to taste
- 1 cup marinara sauce
- 2 cups shredded mozzarella cheese
- 1/2 cup grated Parmesan cheese
- Olive oil for frying

Instructions:
1. Preheat the oven to 375°F (190°C).
2. Place the flour, beaten eggs, and breadcrumbs in separate shallow dishes. Season the breadcrumbs with dried oregano, dried basil, salt, and black pepper.
3. Dip each eggplant slice into the flour, shaking off excess, then into the beaten eggs, and finally coat with breadcrumbs. Ensure each slice is evenly coated.
4. In a large skillet, heat olive oil over medium heat. Fry the coated eggplant slices until golden brown on both sides. Place them on paper towels to absorb excess oil.
5. In a baking dish, spread a thin layer of marinara sauce. Arrange a layer of fried eggplant slices on top. Sprinkle with mozzarella and Parmesan cheese. Repeat the layers, finishing with a generous layer of cheese on top.

6. Bake in the preheated oven for 30-40 minutes or until the cheese is bubbly and golden brown.
7. Allow the Eggplant Parmesan to rest for a few minutes before serving.

Nutrition Information (per serving):
- Calories: 380
- Total Fat: 18g
- Saturated Fat: 9g
- Trans Fat: 0g
- Cholesterol: 100mg
- Sodium: 750mg
- Total Carbohydrates: 32g
- Dietary Fiber: 5g
- Sugars: 5g
- Protein: 21g

This Depression-Era Eggplant Parmesan captures the essence of making do with what's available and turning it into a dish that is both economical and delicious, much like the characters in Steinbeck's iconic novel.

89. Oakie Orange Marmalade

Step into the world of "The Grapes of Wrath" by John Steinbeck with a delightful culinary journey inspired by the novel. Among the 102 food ideas, we present the "Oakie Orange Marmalade," a sweet and tangy preserve that captures the essence of resilience and warmth found in the characters of the story. This marmalade is a tribute to the Oakies, the hardworking families who faced adversity during the Great Depression, just like the Joads in Steinbeck's masterpiece. Spread a bit of history on your toast with this flavorful creation!

Serving: Makes approximately 3 cups of marmalade.
Preparation Time: 15 minutes
Ready Time: 2 hours (including cooling time)

Ingredients:
- 4 large navel oranges
- 1 lemon
- 4 cups granulated sugar

- 1 cinnamon stick
- 1/4 teaspoon ground cloves
- 1/2 teaspoon butter (optional, to reduce foaming)

Instructions:

1. Wash the oranges and lemon thoroughly. Using a sharp knife, thinly slice the oranges and lemon, removing seeds as you go. You can choose to leave the peel on for a chunkier marmalade or peel them for a smoother texture.
2. In a large, heavy-bottomed pot, combine the sliced oranges, lemon, and sugar. Let the mixture sit for about 10 minutes to allow the sugar to draw out the fruit juices.
3. Place the pot over medium heat, stirring until the sugar has completely dissolved.
4. Add the cinnamon stick, ground cloves, and butter (if using) to the pot. Stir well.
5. Bring the mixture to a boil, then reduce the heat to low and let it simmer uncovered for about 1.5 to 2 hours. Stir occasionally to prevent sticking.
6. Check the marmalade's consistency by placing a small amount on a cold plate. If it wrinkles when touched, it's ready. If not, continue simmering and test again every 15 minutes.
7. Once the marmalade reaches the desired consistency, remove it from the heat. Remove the cinnamon stick and discard.
8. Allow the marmalade to cool for about 15 minutes before ladling it into sterilized jars.
9. Seal the jars tightly and let them cool to room temperature. Store in the refrigerator.

Nutrition Information:
(Per 1 tablespoon serving)
- Calories: 50
- Total Fat: 0g
- Cholesterol: 0mg
- Sodium: 0mg
- Total Carbohydrates: 13g
- Dietary Fiber: 0.5g
- Sugars: 12g
- Protein: 0g

Enjoy the Oakie Orange Marmalade on your morning toast or as a delightful accompaniment to cheeses. Let the flavors transport you to the heart of Steinbeck's Dust Bowl era while savoring a taste of perseverance and hope.

90. Sourdough Sushi

In the heart of hardship, creativity blooms. Inspired by the resilient spirit of John Steinbeck's "The Grapes of Wrath," this recipe for Sourdough Sushi embodies resourcefulness and adaptation. Combining the essence of traditional sushi with the tangy allure of sourdough, it's a testament to innovation born from necessity.

Serving: Serves: 4-6 people
Preparation Time: 30 minutes (plus sourdough starter prep time)
Ready Time: Ready in: 2-3 days (including sourdough fermentation)

Ingredients:
- For the Sourdough Starter:
- 1 cup all-purpose flour
- 1 cup water
- For the Sourdough Sushi Rice:
- 2 cups sushi rice
- 2 1/2 cups water
- 1/4 cup rice vinegar
- 2 tablespoons sugar
- 1 teaspoon salt
- For Sourdough Sushi Fillings (Choose any combination):
- Sliced fresh vegetables (cucumber, avocado, bell peppers)
- Cooked and seasoned proteins (grilled chicken, smoked salmon, tofu)
- Condiments like mayonnaise, sriracha, or soy sauce
- Optional: Nori sheets (seaweed) for wrapping

Instructions:
1. Prepare the Sourdough Starter:
- Mix 1 cup of flour and 1 cup of water in a glass or ceramic bowl until combined.

- Cover loosely with a clean cloth and let it sit in a warm area for 24-48 hours, stirring occasionally, until it becomes bubbly and slightly sour.

2. Make the Sourdough Sushi Rice:

- Rinse sushi rice in cold water until the water runs clear. Cook the rice with 2 1/2 cups of water in a rice cooker or on the stove.

- In a small saucepan, combine rice vinegar, sugar, and salt. Heat gently, stirring until the sugar and salt dissolve. Let it cool.

- Once the rice is cooked, transfer it to a large bowl and gently fold in the vinegar mixture. Let it cool to room temperature.

3. Prepare the Fillings:

- Slice vegetables and proteins into thin strips for easy rolling. Season proteins as desired.

4. Assemble the Sourdough Sushi:

- Lay a sheet of plastic wrap on a clean surface. Place a layer of the prepared sourdough starter evenly over the plastic wrap.

- Spread a layer of sushi rice over the sourdough starter, leaving a small border around the edges.

- Arrange fillings in a line along the edge closest to you.

- Using the plastic wrap, carefully roll the sushi tightly, applying gentle pressure to seal.

- Repeat with remaining ingredients.

5. Slice and Serve:

- With a sharp knife, slice the sushi rolls into even pieces.

- Arrange on a serving platter and serve with soy sauce, wasabi, or other preferred condiments.

Nutrition Information (per serving):
(Note: Nutritional values may vary based on chosen fillings)
- Calories: Approximately 250-300 calories per 6-piece serving
- Protein: 5-10 grams
- Carbohydrates: 40-50 grams
- Fat: 2-5 grams
- Fiber: 3-5 grams

This Sourdough Sushi celebrates ingenuity and adaptation, echoing the resourcefulness displayed by characters in Steinbeck's iconic novel. Enjoy this fusion of flavors as a testament to resilience and innovation in challenging times.

91. Vineyard Veggie Vermicelli

In "The Grapes of Wrath," Steinbeck vividly captures the struggles and resilience of those affected by the Dust Bowl. Inspired by the perseverance of the Joad family, this recipe, Vineyard Veggie Vermicelli, celebrates the simplicity and sustenance found in the midst of hardship. With flavors reminiscent of vineyard-fresh produce, it's a nourishing tribute to resilience and resourcefulness.

Serving: 4 servings
Preparation Time: 15 minutes
Ready Time: 25 minutes

Ingredients:
- 8 oz vermicelli noodles
- 2 tablespoons olive oil
- 3 cloves garlic, minced
- 1 onion, thinly sliced
- 1 red bell pepper, thinly sliced
- 1 yellow bell pepper, thinly sliced
- 1 zucchini, thinly sliced
- 1 cup cherry tomatoes, halved
- 1 teaspoon dried oregano
- 1 teaspoon dried basil
- Salt and pepper to taste
- Grated Parmesan cheese for garnish (optional)
- Fresh basil leaves for garnish (optional)

Instructions:
1. Cook the vermicelli noodles according to the package instructions. Drain and set aside.
2. Heat olive oil in a large skillet over medium heat. Add minced garlic and sauté for 1 minute until fragrant.
3. Add sliced onion to the skillet and cook until translucent, about 2 minutes.
4. Toss in the sliced red and yellow bell peppers, stirring occasionally until they begin to soften, approximately 3-4 minutes.
5. Add the thinly sliced zucchini to the skillet and cook for an additional 2-3 minutes until slightly tender.

6. Incorporate the halved cherry tomatoes, dried oregano, dried basil, salt, and pepper. Stir well to combine and cook for another 2 minutes.
7. Gently fold in the cooked vermicelli noodles, ensuring they are well coated with the vegetable mixture. Cook for an additional 2-3 minutes to heat through.
8. Remove from heat and garnish with grated Parmesan cheese and fresh basil leaves, if desired, before serving.

Nutrition Information:
(Note: Nutritional values may vary based on specific ingredients used and serving sizes.)
- Calories per serving: Approximately 320
- Total fat: 7g
- Cholesterol: 0mg
- Sodium: 12mg
- Total carbohydrates: 56g
- Dietary fiber: 4g
- Sugars: 5g
- Protein: 9g

This Vineyard Veggie Vermicelli combines the essence of fresh vegetables with aromatic herbs, offering a hearty dish that pays homage to the enduring spirit depicted in Steinbeck's classic novel.

92. Route 66 Radicchio Wraps

Embark on a culinary journey reminiscent of the Dust Bowl era with these "Route 66 Radicchio Wraps," inspired by John Steinbeck's epic novel, "The Grapes of Wrath." In the spirit of resilience and resourcefulness, these wraps bring together fresh, vibrant ingredients that pay homage to the resilience of the characters in Steinbeck's masterpiece. Get ready to savor the flavors of the open road with this simple yet flavorful recipe.

Serving: Makes 4 servings
Preparation Time: 15 minutes
Ready Time: 30 minutes

Ingredients:

- 8 large radicchio leaves (as the wrap base)
- 1 pound ground turkey or plant-based alternative
- 1 tablespoon olive oil
- 1 onion, finely chopped
- 2 cloves garlic, minced
- 1 teaspoon ground cumin
- 1 teaspoon chili powder
- Salt and pepper to taste
- 1 cup cooked quinoa
- 1 cup black beans, drained and rinsed
- 1 cup corn kernels (fresh or frozen)
- 1 cup cherry tomatoes, diced
- 1 avocado, sliced
- 1/2 cup cilantro, chopped
- Juice of 1 lime

Instructions:
1. Prepare the Radicchio Leaves:
Gently wash and dry the radicchio leaves. Carefully remove them from the head, keeping them intact to serve as the wraps.
2. Cook the Ground Turkey (or plant-based alternative):
In a large skillet, heat olive oil over medium heat. Add chopped onions and garlic, sautéing until softened. Add the ground turkey (or plant-based alternative) and cook until browned. Season with cumin, chili powder, salt, and pepper.
3. Assemble the Filling:
Stir in the cooked quinoa, black beans, corn, and diced cherry tomatoes into the skillet with the cooked turkey. Mix well and let it cook for an additional 5 minutes until flavors meld.
4. Prepare the Wraps:
Spoon the filling onto each radicchio leaf. Top with avocado slices and a sprinkle of chopped cilantro. Squeeze lime juice over the top for a burst of freshness.
5. Roll and Secure:
Carefully roll each radicchio leaf around the filling, creating a wrap. Secure with toothpicks if needed.
6. Serve:
Arrange the Route 66 Radicchio Wraps on a platter and serve immediately.

Nutrition Information:
(Per serving)
- Calories: 350
- Protein: 20g
- Carbohydrates: 35g
- Dietary Fiber: 9g
- Sugars: 4g
- Total Fat: 16g
- Saturated Fat: 3g
- Cholesterol: 40mg
- Sodium: 280mg
- Vitamin D: 0mcg
- Calcium: 70mg
- Iron: 4mg
- Potassium: 870mg

Experience the flavors of hardship and triumph with these Route 66 Radicchio Wraps – a delicious tribute to the enduring spirit of The Grapes of Wrath. Enjoy this dish as a reminder that even in the face of adversity, there's always room for a satisfying and nourishing meal.

93. Joad Family Focaccia

Step back in time and savor the flavors of the Dust Bowl era with the Joad Family Focaccia, a humble yet hearty bread inspired by John Steinbeck's classic novel, "The Grapes of Wrath." This simple and rustic recipe reflects the resourcefulness and resilience of the Joad family as they navigated the challenges of the Great Depression. Embark on a culinary journey through history as you recreate this timeless focaccia, bringing the spirit of Steinbeck's characters to life in your kitchen.

Serving: 8-10 servings
Preparation Time: 15 minutes
Ready Time: 2 hours (including rising time)

Ingredients:
- 1 1/2 cups warm water (110°F/43°C)
- 2 teaspoons sugar
- 2 1/4 teaspoons active dry yeast

- 4 cups all-purpose flour
- 1 teaspoon salt
- 1/2 cup olive oil (divided)
- 2 tablespoons fresh rosemary, chopped
- Coarse sea salt for sprinkling

Instructions:

1. In a small bowl, combine warm water and sugar. Sprinkle yeast over the water and let it sit for 5-10 minutes until it becomes frothy.
2. In a large mixing bowl, combine the flour and salt. Make a well in the center and pour in the yeast mixture and 1/4 cup of olive oil. Mix until a dough forms.
3. Knead the dough on a floured surface for about 5-7 minutes, or until it becomes smooth and elastic.
4. Place the dough in a lightly oiled bowl, cover it with a damp cloth, and let it rise in a warm place for 1 hour, or until it doubles in size.
5. Preheat the oven to 425°F (220°C). Punch down the risen dough and transfer it to a greased baking sheet, pressing it out to the edges.
6. Using your fingers, create dimples in the dough's surface. Drizzle the remaining olive oil over the top, making sure it fills the dimples. Sprinkle chopped rosemary and coarse sea salt evenly.
7. Allow the dough to rest for an additional 30 minutes to rise a bit more.
8. Bake in the preheated oven for 20-25 minutes or until golden brown.
9. Cool slightly before slicing and serving.

Nutrition Information:

Note: Nutrition information is approximate and may vary based on specific ingredients and portion sizes.
- Calories: 250 per serving
- Fat: 10g
- Saturated Fat: 1.5g
- Cholesterol: 0mg
- Sodium: 300mg
- Carbohydrates: 35g
- Fiber: 2g
- Sugars: 1g
- Protein: 5g

Delight in the warm, comforting aroma of the Joad Family Focaccia, a dish that pays homage to the endurance and unity of the Joads in Steinbeck's unforgettable tale.

94. Tractor Trail Taco Salad

In the spirit of John Steinbeck's iconic novel, "The Grapes of Wrath," we present the Tractor Trail Taco Salad—a hearty and flavorful dish inspired by the resilience and resourcefulness of the Joad family as they journeyed through the Dust Bowl era. This taco salad pays homage to the hardworking spirit of those who faced adversity with strength and determination. With a blend of fresh ingredients and bold flavors, the Tractor Trail Taco Salad is a satisfying culinary journey that captures the essence of the novel's enduring themes.

Serving: 4 servings
Preparation Time: 15 minutes
Ready Time: 25 minutes

Ingredients:
- 1 lb ground beef or plant-based alternative
- 1 tablespoon olive oil
- 1 onion, finely chopped
- 2 cloves garlic, minced
- 1 packet taco seasoning
- 1 can (15 oz) black beans, drained and rinsed
- 1 cup corn kernels (fresh or frozen)
- 1 cup cherry tomatoes, halved
- 1 cup shredded lettuce
- 1 cup shredded cheddar cheese
- 1 avocado, diced
- 1/2 cup sliced black olives
- 1/4 cup chopped fresh cilantro
- 1 cup tortilla chips, crushed
- 1/2 cup sour cream (optional)
- Lime wedges for garnish

Instructions:
1. In a large skillet, heat the olive oil over medium heat. Add the chopped onions and garlic, sautéing until softened.

2. Add the ground beef or plant-based alternative to the skillet, breaking it apart with a spatula as it cooks. Cook until browned.

3. Stir in the taco seasoning, black beans, and corn. Cook for an additional 5-7 minutes, allowing the flavors to meld.

4. While the mixture is cooking, prepare the fresh ingredients: chop the tomatoes, shred the lettuce, dice the avocado, and gather the remaining toppings.

5. Assemble the taco salad by layering the shredded lettuce on a large serving platter or individual plates. Top with the cooked meat mixture.

6. Sprinkle the cherry tomatoes, shredded cheddar cheese, diced avocado, black olives, and fresh cilantro over the meat mixture.

7. Finish by generously scattering crushed tortilla chips over the top for added crunch.

8. Optional: Drizzle with sour cream and garnish with lime wedges for a burst of citrus.

9. Serve immediately, allowing everyone to mix the ingredients together or customize their portions.

Nutrition Information:
(Per serving)
- Calories: 550
- Protein: 28g
- Fat: 32g
- Carbohydrates: 40g
- Fiber: 10g
- Sugar: 5g
- Sodium: 800mg

Indulge in the Tractor Trail Taco Salad—a tribute to the enduring spirit and flavors of a journey inspired by "The Grapes of Wrath."

95. Bankrupt Beet Borscht

In the spirit of John Steinbeck's "The Grapes of Wrath," a novel that vividly portrays the struggles of the Dust Bowl era, we present the "Bankrupt Beet Borscht." This hearty and flavorful beet soup pays homage to the endurance of those who faced economic hardship and displacement. The deep, earthy hues of the beets symbolize the resilience of the human spirit, making this dish a fitting addition to our collection of recipes inspired by Steinbeck's iconic work.

Serving: 4-6 servings
Preparation Time: 20 minutes
Ready Time: 1 hour

Ingredients:
- 4 medium-sized beets, peeled and grated
- 1 onion, finely chopped
- 2 carrots, peeled and grated
- 2 potatoes, peeled and diced
- 3 cloves garlic, minced
- 1 can (15 oz) diced tomatoes
- 4 cups vegetable broth
- 1 tablespoon olive oil
- 2 bay leaves
- 1 teaspoon caraway seeds
- Salt and pepper to taste
- 2 tablespoons red wine vinegar
- Sour cream and fresh dill for garnish

Instructions:
1. Prepare the Vegetables:
- Peel and grate the beets.
- Finely chop the onion.
- Peel and grate the carrots.
- Peel and dice the potatoes.
- Mince the garlic.
2. Sauté the Vegetables:
- In a large pot, heat olive oil over medium heat.
- Add chopped onions and sauté until translucent.
- Add minced garlic and sauté for an additional minute.
3. Add Beets and Carrots:
- Stir in grated beets and carrots, cooking for 5 minutes to soften.
4. Add Potatoes and Tomatoes:
- Add diced potatoes, canned tomatoes (with juice), and vegetable broth.
- Bring the mixture to a boil, then reduce heat to simmer.
5. Season and Simmer:
- Add bay leaves, caraway seeds, salt, and pepper.

- Cover and simmer for 45 minutes to allow flavors to meld.
6. Finish and Serve:
- Stir in red wine vinegar for a touch of acidity.
- Remove bay leaves and discard.
- Ladle the borscht into bowls, and garnish with a dollop of sour cream and fresh dill.

Nutrition Information:
Note: Nutritional values are approximate and may vary based on specific ingredients used.
- Calories per serving: 180
- Total Fat: 4g
- Saturated Fat: 1g
- Cholesterol: 0mg
- Sodium: 800mg
- Total Carbohydrates: 32g
- Dietary Fiber: 6g
- Sugars: 10g
- Protein: 4g
Warm and nourishing, the "Bankrupt Beet Borscht" invites you to savor the essence of survival, reflecting the strength found in simple, humble ingredients. Enjoy this comforting bowl of borscht as a tribute to the indomitable spirit of those who weathered the storms of life during the Dust Bowl era.

96. Peach Pit Pasta Primavera

In "The Grapes of Wrath," John Steinbeck evokes the resilience of the human spirit amidst adversity. Inspired by the novel's themes of resourcefulness and sustenance, this Peach Pit Pasta Primavera is a tribute to making the most of what's available, creating a dish that celebrates flavor and ingenuity.

Serving: 4 servings
Preparation Time: 15 minutes
Ready Time: 30 minutes

Ingredients:

- 12 ounces pasta (linguine or spaghetti)
- 2 cups fresh or frozen peas
- 2 tablespoons olive oil
- 4 cloves garlic, minced
- 1 onion, thinly sliced
- 2 carrots, julienned
- 1 bell pepper, thinly sliced
- 1 cup sliced mushrooms
- Salt and pepper to taste
- 4 ripe peaches, pits removed and diced
- 1/4 cup fresh basil, chopped
- Grated Parmesan cheese (optional)

Instructions:

1. Prepare Pasta: Cook pasta according to package instructions in a pot of salted boiling water until al dente. In the last 3 minutes of cooking, add the peas. Drain and set aside.
2. Sauté Vegetables: In a large skillet, heat olive oil over medium heat. Add minced garlic and sauté for a minute until fragrant. Add sliced onion, julienned carrots, bell pepper, and mushrooms. Cook, stirring occasionally, until the vegetables are tender, about 5-7 minutes.
3. Season and Add Peaches: Season the vegetable mix with salt and pepper to taste. Add diced peaches and continue to cook for an additional 2-3 minutes until the peaches are warmed through but still firm.
4. Combine Pasta and Vegetables: Add the cooked pasta and peas to the skillet with the peach and vegetable mix. Toss everything together gently until well combined and heated through.
5. Finish and Serve: Remove from heat and sprinkle chopped basil over the pasta. Serve hot, garnished with grated Parmesan cheese if desired.

Nutrition Information:

Note: Nutritional values may vary based on specific ingredients used and serving sizes.
- Calories: Approximately 400 per serving
- Fat: 8g
- Carbohydrates: 70g
- Protein: 13g
- Fiber: 9g

This Peach Pit Pasta Primavera captures the essence of resourcefulness and adaptability, offering a delightful blend of flavors and textures that resonate with the spirit of making the most out of what's available—a perfect homage to the enduring themes in Steinbeck's masterpiece.

97. Weedpatch Walnut Butter

'Weedpatch Walnut Butter" pays homage to the resilient spirit of the Joad family and the community they found at Weedpatch Camp in John Steinbeck's "The Grapes of Wrath." This nutty, wholesome spread encapsulates the simplicity and strength found in the midst of hardship.

Serving: - Makes approximately 1 cup of Weedpatch Walnut Butter
Preparation Time: - 10 minutes
Ready Time: - 15 minutes

Ingredients:
- 2 cups walnuts, raw and unsalted
- 2 tablespoons honey or maple syrup
- 1 teaspoon cinnamon
- 1/4 teaspoon salt (adjust to taste)
- Optional: 1-2 tablespoons walnut oil (for a creamier texture)

Instructions:
1. Preheat Oven: Preheat your oven to 350°F (175°C).
2. Toast Walnuts: Spread the walnuts evenly on a baking sheet and toast them in the preheated oven for 8-10 minutes, or until they become fragrant. Be careful not to burn them; stir occasionally.
3. Cool Walnuts: Allow the toasted walnuts to cool for a few minutes until they are warm but not hot.
4. Blend Walnuts: Place the cooled walnuts in a food processor. Add honey or maple syrup, cinnamon, and salt.
5. Blend until Smooth: Blend the ingredients, scraping down the sides occasionally, until the mixture turns into a smooth, creamy butter. This process might take a few minutes. If the mixture seems too thick, add walnut oil gradually until desired consistency is reached.
6. Taste and Adjust: Taste the walnut butter and adjust sweetness or saltiness as per your preference.

7. Store: Transfer the Weedpatch Walnut Butter to a clean, airtight jar. It can be stored in the refrigerator for up to two weeks.

Nutrition Information (per 1 tablespoon serving):
- Calories: 94
- Total Fat: 9g
- Saturated Fat: 1g
- Sodium: 29mg
- Total Carbohydrates: 3g
- Dietary Fiber: 1g
- Sugars: 1g
- Protein: 2g

This Weedpatch Walnut Butter serves as a delightful spread on toast, as an ingredient in baking, or simply enjoyed by the spoonful. Its rich, earthy flavor mirrors the resilience and warmth found in the story of "The Grapes of Wrath."

98. Oakie Oregano Oysters

'Oakie Oregano Oysters" pays homage to the resilience and resourcefulness of the characters in John Steinbeck's "The Grapes of Wrath." This dish embodies the spirit of making the most of what's available, combining the brininess of oysters with the earthy allure of oregano, reminiscent of the flavors cherished during times of scarcity.

Serving: 4 servings
Preparation time: 15 minutes
Ready time: 30 minutes

Ingredients:
- 16 fresh oysters, shucked
- 1/2 cup breadcrumbs
- 2 tablespoons butter, melted
- 2 cloves garlic, minced
- 1 teaspoon dried oregano
- 1/4 teaspoon black pepper
- 1/4 teaspoon salt
- 1 lemon, cut into wedges for garnish

- Fresh parsley, chopped (for garnish)

Instructions:
1. Preheat your oven to 425°F (220°C). Place the shucked oysters on a baking sheet lined with parchment paper or in a shallow baking dish.
2. In a mixing bowl, combine the breadcrumbs, melted butter, minced garlic, dried oregano, black pepper, and salt. Mix well until the ingredients are evenly incorporated.
3. Spoon a generous amount of the breadcrumb mixture onto each oyster, ensuring they are evenly coated.
4. Place the baking sheet or dish in the preheated oven and bake for 10-12 minutes or until the breadcrumbs turn golden brown and the edges of the oysters start to curl.
5. Once done, remove from the oven and garnish with freshly chopped parsley. Serve hot with lemon wedges on the side.

Nutrition Information:
(Note: Nutrition Information can vary based on specific ingredients and serving sizes. Here's an approximate per serving breakdown.)
- Calories: 170
- Total Fat: 8g
- Saturated Fat: 4g
- Trans Fat: 0g
- Cholesterol: 50mg
- Sodium: 380mg
- Total Carbohydrate: 14g
- Dietary Fiber: 1g
- Sugars: 1g
- Protein: 10g
This dish celebrates the simple yet robust flavors that resonate with the themes of resilience and making do with what's available, much like the characters in "The Grapes of Wrath."

99. Depression Dal Dip

In the spirit of John Steinbeck's classic novel, "The Grapes of Wrath," we present the Depression Dal Dip—a comforting and hearty dish that pays homage to the resilience of the human spirit in the face of adversity.

This wholesome dal dip is a fusion of flavors inspired by the journey of the Joad family, reflecting the simple yet profound essence of survival during challenging times.

Serving: Serves 4
Preparation Time: 15 minutes
Ready Time: 45 minutes

Ingredients:
- 1 cup red lentils, washed and drained
- 2 cups water
- 2 tablespoons olive oil
- 1 onion, finely chopped
- 3 cloves garlic, minced
- 1 teaspoon ground cumin
- 1 teaspoon ground coriander
- 1/2 teaspoon turmeric powder
- 1/2 teaspoon paprika
- 1 can (14 oz) diced tomatoes, undrained
- Salt and pepper to taste
- 1 tablespoon lemon juice
- 2 tablespoons fresh cilantro, chopped (for garnish)
- Greek yogurt or sour cream (optional, for serving)
- Pita bread or tortilla chips (for dipping)

Instructions:
1. In a medium-sized pot, combine the red lentils and water. Bring to a boil, then reduce the heat to simmer. Cook for 15-20 minutes or until lentils are tender.
2. In a separate pan, heat olive oil over medium heat. Add chopped onions and garlic, sautéing until they become translucent.
3. Stir in the ground cumin, ground coriander, turmeric, and paprika. Cook for an additional 2 minutes, allowing the spices to release their flavors.
4. Add the spiced onion mixture to the cooked lentils. Pour in the diced tomatoes with their juice. Season with salt and pepper to taste. Simmer for an additional 15-20 minutes, allowing the flavors to meld.
5. Just before serving, stir in the lemon juice for a refreshing zing.
6. Garnish the Depression Dal Dip with chopped cilantro. Optionally, serve with a dollop of Greek yogurt or sour cream on the side.

7. Pair the dip with warm pita bread or tortilla chips for a delightful texture contrast.

Nutrition Information:
(Per Serving)
- Calories: 220
- Protein: 12g
- Fat: 7g
- Carbohydrates: 30g
- Fiber: 10g
- Sugar: 3g
- Sodium: 480mg

Embrace the flavors of hope and perseverance with this Depression Dal Dip, a dish that captures the essence of survival and community in challenging times.

100. Grapes of Wrath Gingersnaps

Celebrate the flavors of The Grapes of Wrath with these delightful "Grapes of Wrath Gingersnaps." Inspired by the resilience and strength of the Joad family, these cookies blend the warmth of traditional gingersnaps with a hint of sweetness reminiscent of the hope that prevails even in the toughest times. Perfect for sharing with loved ones, these cookies are a tribute to the enduring spirit of the human soul.

Serving: Makes approximately 24 cookies
Preparation Time: 15 minutes
Ready Time: 45 minutes

Ingredients:
- 2 1/4 cups all-purpose flour
- 1 teaspoon baking soda
- 1/2 teaspoon salt
- 1 1/2 teaspoons ground ginger
- 1 1/2 teaspoons ground cinnamon
- 1/2 teaspoon ground cloves
- 3/4 cup unsalted butter, softened
- 1 cup granulated sugar

- 1/4 cup molasses
- 1 large egg
- 1/2 cup finely chopped raisins
- 1/4 cup finely chopped walnuts (optional)
- Additional granulated sugar for rolling

Instructions:
1. Preheat the oven:
Preheat your oven to 350°F (175°C) and line baking sheets with parchment paper.
2. Combine dry ingredients:
In a medium bowl, whisk together the flour, baking soda, salt, ginger, cinnamon, and cloves. Set aside.
3. Cream the butter and sugar:
In a large bowl, cream together the softened butter and granulated sugar until light and fluffy.
4. Add wet ingredients:
Beat in the molasses and egg until well combined.
5. Incorporate dry ingredients:
Gradually add the dry ingredient mixture to the wet ingredients, mixing until just combined.
6. Fold in raisins and walnuts:
Gently fold in the finely chopped raisins and walnuts (if using) until evenly distributed throughout the dough.
7. Shape into balls:
Take tablespoon-sized portions of dough and roll them into balls. Roll each ball in additional granulated sugar to coat.
8. Place on baking sheets:
Arrange the sugar-coated dough balls on the prepared baking sheets, leaving space between each cookie.
9. Bake:
Bake in the preheated oven for 10-12 minutes or until the edges are lightly golden. The cookies will continue to firm up as they cool.
10. Cool and enjoy:
Allow the cookies to cool on the baking sheets for a few minutes before transferring them to a wire rack to cool completely.

Nutrition Information:
Note: Nutritional values are per cookie.
- Calories: 120

- Total Fat: 6g
- Saturated Fat: 3.5g
- Cholesterol: 20mg
- Sodium: 85mg
- Total Carbohydrates: 16g
- Sugars: 9g
- Protein: 1g

These "Grapes of Wrath Gingersnaps" offer a taste of comfort and resilience—a perfect treat to accompany moments of reflection and connection inspired by John Steinbeck's classic novel.

101. Okie Olive Loaf

Embark on a culinary journey inspired by John Steinbeck's iconic novel, "The Grapes of Wrath," with the hearty and flavorful "Okie Olive Loaf." This dish pays homage to the resilience and resourcefulness of the Okie community during the Dust Bowl era. Just as the Joad family navigated challenges with determination, this dish combines simple ingredients to create a delicious and satisfying loaf that brings people together at the table.

Serving: Makes one loaf, approximately 8 servings.
Preparation Time: 15 minutes
Ready Time: 1 hour 15 minutes

Ingredients:
- 2 cups all-purpose flour
- 1 tablespoon baking powder
- 1 teaspoon salt
- 1/2 cup black olives, chopped
- 1/2 cup green olives, chopped
- 1/2 cup red bell pepper, finely diced
- 1/2 cup green bell pepper, finely diced
- 1/2 cup onion, finely diced
- 1 cup sharp cheddar cheese, shredded
- 2 large eggs
- 1 cup milk
- 1/4 cup olive oil

- 1 tablespoon honey

Instructions:
1. Preheat your oven to 350°F (175°C). Grease a loaf pan and set it aside.
2. In a large mixing bowl, combine the flour, baking powder, and salt.
3. Add the black olives, green olives, red bell pepper, green bell pepper, onion, and cheddar cheese to the dry ingredients. Mix well until the ingredients are evenly distributed.
4. In a separate bowl, whisk together the eggs, milk, olive oil, and honey.
5. Pour the wet ingredients into the dry ingredients and stir until just combined. Be careful not to overmix; a few lumps are okay.
6. Pour the batter into the prepared loaf pan, spreading it evenly.
7. Bake in the preheated oven for 1 hour or until a toothpick inserted into the center comes out clean.
8. Allow the Okie Olive Loaf to cool in the pan for 10 minutes before transferring it to a wire rack to cool completely.
9. Once cooled, slice and serve. This loaf is delicious on its own or accompanied by a spread of butter or cream cheese.

Nutrition Information:
Note: Nutritional values are approximate and may vary based on specific ingredients used.
- Calories per serving: 240
- Total Fat: 11g
- Saturated Fat: 4g
- Trans Fat: 0g
- Cholesterol: 52mg
- Sodium: 540mg
- Total Carbohydrates: 27g
- Dietary Fiber: 2g
- Sugars: 4g
- Protein: 9g

Indulge in the rustic charm of the Okie Olive Loaf, a savory creation that captures the essence of survival, community, and the enduring spirit of the human soul – a perfect addition to your journey through the flavors inspired by "The Grapes of Wrath."

102. Tomato Tin Tiramisu

Step into the world of "The Grapes of Wrath" with a culinary twist – Tomato Tin Tiramisu. Inspired by the resilience and resourcefulness of the Joad family, this unique dessert transforms the humble tomato tin into a delightful tiramisu. Drawing inspiration from the novel's depiction of hardship and triumph, this recipe combines unexpected ingredients to create a surprisingly delicious treat.

Serving: Serves 8
Preparation Time: 20 minutes
Ready Time: 4 hours (including chilling time)

Ingredients:
- 1 can (28 oz) crushed tomatoes
- 1 cup strong brewed coffee, cooled
- 1 cup granulated sugar
- 4 large eggs, separated
- 1 teaspoon vanilla extract
- 8 ounces mascarpone cheese, softened
- 24 to 30 ladyfinger cookies
- Cocoa powder for dusting
- Fresh mint leaves for garnish (optional)

Instructions:
1. Prepare the Tomato Tin:
- Drain the crushed tomatoes, reserving the juice for another use.
- Clean and dry the tomato tin thoroughly.
2. Brew Coffee:
- Brew a strong cup of coffee and let it cool to room temperature.
3. Tomato Tin Layer:
- Line the bottom of the tomato tin with ladyfinger cookies, creating the first layer.
4. Coffee Soak:
- In a shallow dish, mix the cooled coffee with 1/2 cup of granulated sugar until dissolved.
- Gently dip each ladyfinger into the coffee mixture, ensuring they are well-soaked but not overly saturated.
5. Mascarpone Mixture:

- In a bowl, beat the egg yolks with the remaining sugar until pale and creamy.
- Add vanilla extract and mascarpone cheese, blending until smooth.
6. Egg Whites:
- In a separate clean, dry bowl, whip the egg whites until stiff peaks form.
7. Folding:
- Gently fold the whipped egg whites into the mascarpone mixture, creating a light and airy texture.
8. Layering:
- Pour half of the mascarpone mixture over the ladyfinger layer in the tomato tin.
9. Repeat Layers:
- Add another layer of soaked ladyfingers on top of the mascarpone mixture.
- Pour the remaining mascarpone mixture over the second layer of ladyfingers.
10. Chill:
- Cover the tomato tin with plastic wrap and refrigerate for at least 4 hours or overnight, allowing the flavors to meld.
11. Serve:
- Before serving, dust the top with cocoa powder and garnish with fresh mint leaves if desired.

Nutrition Information:
(Per Serving)
- Calories: 320
- Total Fat: 18g
- Saturated Fat: 10g
- Cholesterol: 130mg
- Sodium: 50mg
- Total Carbohydrates: 34g
- Dietary Fiber: 1g
- Sugars: 20g
- Protein: 6g
Celebrate the indomitable spirit of "The Grapes of Wrath" with this Tomato Tin Tiramisu – a dessert that transforms adversity into a triumph for your taste buds.

CONCLUSION

"Dust Bowl Dinners: 102 Culinary Tributes Inspired by The Grapes of Wrath" is not just a cookbook; it's a journey through history and culture, a celebration of resilience and resourcefulness, and a testament to the power of food to connect us to our roots. As we conclude this culinary exploration inspired by John Steinbeck's iconic novel, "The Grapes of Wrath," we find ourselves not only satiated but enriched with a deeper understanding of the human spirit and the role that food plays in shaping our stories.

The 102 food ideas presented in this cookbook serve as more than just recipes; they are culinary tributes to the characters and the era depicted in Steinbeck's masterpiece. Each dish encapsulates the essence of the Dust Bowl era, telling a story of struggle, survival, and the simple joys that brought solace to those enduring hardships. From the humble fare of migrant camps to the rare indulgences that provided a brief escape from adversity, these recipes are a flavorful homage to the resilience of the Joad family and their fellow travelers.

In our exploration, we encountered dishes that mirrored the scarcity of resources during the Dust Bowl. From the inventive use of basic ingredients to create hearty meals, such as the Panhandle Pinto Stew or Okie Cornbread, to the clever repurposing of leftovers in the Depression Casserole, these recipes transport us to a time when necessity was the mother of culinary invention. Through these culinary creations, we gain a taste of the resourcefulness that sustained families during an era marked by hardship and deprivation.

The cookbook also pays homage to the communal spirit that defined life in migrant camps. The Campfire Beans and Skillet Cornbread, inspired by the gatherings around shared fires, evoke a sense of community that transcends the limitations of meager provisions. These recipes remind us that, even in the face of adversity, the act of breaking bread together has the power to forge connections and offer a semblance of normalcy in the most challenging circumstances.

Furthermore, "Dust Bowl Dinners" delves into the regional influences that shaped the culinary landscape of the Dust Bowl era. From the Southwestern flavors of the Jalapeño Corn Pudding to the heartiness of Midwestern Meatloaf, each dish reflects the diverse cultural tapestry of the migrants seeking a better life in California. This culinary diversity is a testament to the resilience and adaptability of individuals forced to leave

176

their homes and traditions behind.

As we bid farewell to the pages of "Dust Bowl Dinners," we carry with us not only a collection of recipes but a profound appreciation for the role of food in preserving and sharing the stories of our past. The culinary tributes inspired by "The Grapes of Wrath" serve as a bridge between literature and gastronomy, connecting us to a pivotal period in American history. Through these 102 food ideas, we have tasted the flavors of survival, ingenuity, and hope that sustained the Joad family and countless others during the challenging times of the Dust Bowl era. May these recipes continue to be a source of inspiration, allowing us to savor not only the flavors of the past but also the enduring spirit of those who faced adversity with resilience and courage.

www.ingramcontent.com/pod-product-compliance
Lightning Source LLC
Chambersburg PA
CBHW062250180525
26901CB00011B/1215